# CONTROLLING STRESS
# IN CHILDREN

# CONTROLLING STRESS IN CHILDREN

*By*

## JAMES H. HUMPHREY, Ed.D.

*Professor Emeritus*
*University of Maryland*

*and*

## JOY N. HUMPHREY, M.S.

*Child Stress Management Consultant*
*Wayne County, Michigan*

CHARLES C THOMAS • PUBLISHER
*Springfield • Illinois • U.S.A.*

*Published and Distributed Throughout the World by*

CHARLES C THOMAS • PUBLISHER
2600 South First Street
Springfield, Illinois 62717

© *1985 by* CHARLES C THOMAS • PUBLISHER

ISBN 0-398-05050-3

Library of Congress Catalog Card Number: 84-8651

*With* THOMAS BOOKS *careful attention is given to all details of manufacturing and
design. It is the Publisher's desire to present books that are satisfactory as to their physical
qualities and artistic possibilities and appropriate for their particular use.* THOMAS
BOOKS *will be true to those laws of quality that assure a good name and good will.*

*Printed in the United States of America*
*SC-R-3*

**Library of Congress Cataloging in Publication Data**

Humphrey, James Harry, 1911–
   Controlling stress in children.

   Bibliography: p.
   Includes index.
   1. Stress in children.   2. Parent and child.   3. Child
rearing.   4. Classroom management.   5. Interaction
analysis in education.   6. Children—Counseling of.
I. Humphrey, Joy N.   II. Title.
BF723.S75H845   1984       155.4       84-8651
ISBN 0-398-05050-3

# PREFACE

The last decade has seen a plethora of books and magazine articles published in the area of stress. This no doubt attests to the notion that this area of health concern may well be one of the most important in modern times. It is interesting to note, however, that this abundance of literature has pertained essentially to the adult population. That is, it has appeared generally that stress is mainly concerned only with adults.

With recent discoveries indicating that stress among adults is likely to have its roots in childhood, more attention is currently being directed toward control of stress in children. Our good friend, the late Hans Selye, often referred to as the "Father of Stress," and with whom we have collaborated on certain aspects of childhood stress research once pointed this up in a conversation with us: "I think it is extremely important to begin teaching the stress concept to children at a very early age, because all codes of behavior sink in best if a tradition is established."

This becomes all the more important because it has now been clearly demonstrated that children who associate with adults who are under stress, are very likely to become stress ridden themselves. Herein lies the importance of this book, the purpose of which is to indicate to adults how they can control their own stress and to show them how they can learn to control stress in children.

It is our hope that the book will fill a need in those courses in child development that deal in some way with childhood stress. Also it should serve as a useful reference for parents, teachers, counselors and other adults who are closely associated with children.

James H. Humphrey
Joy N. Humphrey

# INTRODUCTION

This book is directed to those adults who deal in some way with children — parents, teachers, counselors and other adult friends. Its purpose is to help adults themselves understand and to be able to help children understand about stress and how to control it.

Although we tend to think of undesirable stress as being mainly concerned with the adult population, it can have a devastating effect on growing children. If valid information can be provided for adults who deal with children perhaps they will not only be better prepared to understand about stress, but they will be able to take measures to help children control it as well.

The need for a book of this nature is clearly demonstrated by the fact that there is an increasing amount of evidence that shows that children supervised by adults who themselves do not cope well with stress, will pass along to children this same inability to cope. In addition, it has been found that when these same adults improve upon their own ability to control stress, this skill is also passed along to children.

There are so many causes of stress that almost anything that occurs in life can induce stress to some degree. All of the various factors concerned with our modern highly technological society, the mass media, especially the daily news which bombards us with information, overcrowding, air and noise pollution, along with the everyday "hustle and bustle to survive" combine to make life in general a somewhat frustrating experience. All of us, children and adults alike, are possible stress victims of the kinds of conditions mentioned above.

Most children encounter a considerable amount of undesirable stress in our complex modern society. One of the problems of stress in children is that they are not likely to be able to cope with it as well as adults. The reason for this is that they do not have the readily available options that adults might have. In fact, many prominent child psychologists have made the following comparisons between choices in coping with stress open to children and adults.

1. An open display of anger is often considered unacceptable for children. For example, a teacher can be angry with students, but children in turn may not have the same right to be angry with a teacher.
2. Adults can withdraw or walk out, but this same option of freedom is not likely to be available to children.
3. An adult can get a prescription for "nerves" from a physician — another option not available to children.
4. It is very likely that more often than not children may be punished for using some of the same kinds of stress coping techniques that are satisfactory for adults. Yet, some of these behaviors are considered socially unacceptable as far as children are concerned.

Perhaps at this point we should identify the population with which this book is primarily concerned. That is, what do we mean by the term *children*, particularly with reference to age range? In this regard we will deal essentially with children from about age two to about age twelve. Or, from the time children are eligible to enter nursery school until they complete elementary school.

We hasten to mention that stress can occur below two years of age. For example, it is the general belief that infants are unaware of the differences between self and the physical and human environment. Many child development specialists feel that the two most important tasks of the infant and child up to about the age of two are to establish inner images of the outer world of people and objects. In the process of establishing such images life can be unpleasant for this age range and as a result may become stressful.

Finally, it is not absolutely necessary for everyone to be an expert in behavioral therapy in order to deal with stress in childhood. There are certain general principles that most adults can apply in helping to control stress. These principles are presented here to set the stage for a better understanding of the theme and content of the book.

**1. Personal health practices should be carefully observed.** This is an easy principle to accept, but it is not always easy to put into action. No one is against health but not everyone abides by those practices that can help to maintain a suitable level of health. Parents in particular should accept the major share of the responsibility for health practices of children. In doing so, they can help to eliminate unacceptable health behaviors, relating such behaviors to stress.

**2. There should be a continuous effort to take stock of ourselves.** The practice of constantly taking stock of one's activities can help to minimize many problems. This can be accomplished in part by taking a little time at the end of each day for an evaluation of the events that occurred during the day and reactions to those events. Adults should give serious consideration to this practice and attempt to guide children in a direction that will help them understand why they may have become upset over an incident that happened during the day.

**3. Learn to recognize your own accomplishments.** One must learn to recognize his own accomplishments and praise himself for them, especially if such praise is not offered by others. This is generally known as "stroking" or "patting one's self on the back." In practicing this procedure adults can develop positive attitudes and/or belief systems about their own accomplishments and thus reduce stress. At the same time they can try to instill this idea into the lives of children.

**4. Learn to take one thing at a time.** This is concerned with time budgeting and procrastination. Sometimes, both adults and children are likely to put things off, and as a consequence, frustrations can build up as tasks pile up. There is a need to sort out those tasks in order of importance and deal with them one at a time. Proper budgeting of time can help to offset procrastination which itself can be a stress inducing factor. Budgeting of time can help to eliminate worries of time urgency and the feeling of "too much to do in too short a time."

**5. Learn to take things less seriously.** This should not be interpreted to mean that such adult responsibilities as parenting and teaching should not be taken seriously. It does mean that there can be a fine line between what is actually serious and what is not. Sometimes when people look back at a particular event, they may wonder how they could have become so excited about it. Those adults who are able to see the humorous side tend to look at a potentially stressful situation more objectively, and this can assist in keeping stress levels low. This attitude can easily be conveyed to children.

6. **Do things for others.** We can sometimes take our minds off our own stressful conditions by offering to do something for other persons. Children should be taught to develop this concept early in life. When people are helpful to others in attempting to relieve them from stress, they in turn will tend to be relieved of stress themselves. Much research shows that those persons who volunteer to help others often times get as much benefit from this practice as those they volunteer to help. In this regard, it has been clearly demonstrated that older children who have reading problems improve in their own reading ability when they assist younger children with these same problems.

7. **Talk things over with others.** Some individuals tend to keep things to themselves; therefore, they may not be aware that others are disturbed by the same things. Sometimes discussing something with a colleague or with a spouse can help one see things in a much different light. Children should be encouraged to talk things over with each other as well as with parents, teachers and other adult friends.

8. **Stress should not be confused with challenge.** Recognizing that stress is a natural phenomenon of life is no doubt one of the first and most important steps in dealing with it. This is a concept that adults should make every effort to develop with children at an early age.

As you read and acquire information presented in the book it is recommended that you consider these general principles as basic guidelines in directing your efforts to *Controlling Stress in Children*.

# CONTENTS

# CONTROLLING STRESS IN CHILDREN

# CHAPTER 1

# ABOUT STRESS

S TRESS!!! What is it? How do we react to it? What causes it? How does it effect us? Is it all bad? Answers to questions such as these are helpful if adults are to achieve any degree of success in their efforts to control stress in children. That is, they should have some awareness of just what it is they are trying to control. Therefore, it is the function of this initial chapter to provide the reader with an overview of some of the various aspects of stress. A later chapter will be devoted to more specific ways adults can help children themselves understand the complex concept of stress.

## WHAT IS THE MEANING
## OF STRESS—AND OTHER TERMS?

There is no standard meaning of the term *stress* as well as some other terms used in connection with it. For this reason there is a great deal of confusion surrounding its meaning. For example, are stress and anxiety the same? Does stress cause anxiety, or vice versa? Is emotion another word for stress? Does tension bring about stress? And on and on.

Our purpose in identifying and attempting to clarify the meaning of some of these terms is mainly for communication as far as this book is concerned. This is to say that when a term is used, you will know the meaning of it for purposes of this book, and that we are trying to develop working descriptions of terms for the purpose of communicating with you, the reader.

In some instances in the discussion of terms that follow, we will resort to terms used by various authorities in the field and in others, insofar as they may be available, purely technical definitions. It should be understood that many of the terms we will refer to have some sort of general meaning attached to them. An attempt will be made in some cases to start with this general meaning and make it more specific for the subject at hand.

## Stress

There is no solid agreement regarding the derivation of the term stress. Some sources suggest that the term is derived from the Latin word *stringere*, meaning to "bind tightly." Other sources contend that the term derives from the French word *destress* (English — *distress*) and suggest that the prefix "dis" was eventually eliminated because of slurring, as in the case of the word *because* sometimes becoming *'cause*.

A common generalized literal description of the term is a "constraining force or influence." When applied to human beings, this could be interpreted to mean the extent to which the body can withstand a given force or influence. In this regard one of the most often quoted descriptions of stress is that of the late Hans Selye, generally referred to as the "Father of Stress." He described it as the "nonspecific response of the body to any demand made upon it."

This means that stress involves a mobilization of the bodily resources in response to some sort of stimulus. These responses can include various physical and chemical changes in the body. This description of stress could be extended by saying that it involves demands that tax and/or exceed the resources of the human body. This means that stress not only involves these bodily responses, but that it also involves wear and tear on the body brought about by these responses. In essence, stress can be considered as any factor acting internally or externally that makes it difficult to adapt and that induces increased effort on the part of a person to maintain a state of balance within himself and with his external environment. It should be understood that stress is a *state* that one is in, and this should not be confused with any stimulus that produces such a state. These are called *stressors* and will be discussed at various points throughout the book.

## Tension

The term *tension* is very often used in relation to stress and many times it is likely to be confused with it. Tensions can be considered as unnecessary or exaggerated muscle contractions which could be accompanied by abnormally great or reduced activities of the internal organs. We can think about tensions in two ways: first, as *physiologic* or *unlearned* tensions, and second, as *psychologic* or *learned* tensions. An example of the first, unlearned tensions, would be "tensing" at bright lights or intense sounds. Learned tensions are responses to stimuli that ordinarily do not involve muscular contractions, but that at sometime earlier in a person's experiences were associated with a situation in which tension was a part of the normal response. In view of the fact that the brain connects any events that stimulate it simultaneously, it would appear to follow that, depending upon the unlimited kinds of personal experiences one might have had, he may show tension to any and all kinds of stimuli. An example of learned tension would be an inability to relax when riding in a car after experiencing or imagining too many automobile accidents.

In a sense it may be inferred that unlearned tensions are current and spontaneous, while learned tensions may be latent as a result of a previous experience and may emerge at a later time. Although there may be a hairline distinction in the minds of some people, perhaps an essential difference between stress and tension is that the former is a physical and/or mental state concerned with wear and tear on the body, while the latter is either a spontaneous or latent condition that can help to bring about this wear and tear.

## Emotion

Since the terms *stress* and *emotion* are used interchangeably in the literature, it is important that we clarify the meaning of emotion. We like to think of emotion as a response an individual makes when confronted with a situation for which he is unprepared or which he interprets as a possible source of gain or loss for him. For example, if an individual is confronted with a situation for which he may not have a satisfactory response, the emotional pattern of fear could result. Or, if he finds himself in a position where his desires are frustrated, the emotional pattern of anger may occur. Emotion, then, is not the state of stress itself but rather it is a stressor that can stimulate stress. (The subject of emotions will be discussed in detail in a later chapter.)

### Anxiety

Another term often used to mean the same thing as stress is *anxiety.* In fact, some of the literature uses the expression "anxiety *or* stress," implying that they are one and the same thing. This can lead to the "chicken and egg" controversy. That is, is stress the cause of anxiety or is anxiety the cause of stress? Or, is it a reciprocal situation?

A basic literal meaning of the term anxiety is *uneasiness of the mind,* but this simple generalization may be more complex than one might think. Even clinical psychologists who deal with this area sometimes have difficulty defining the term. Some consider it to be the reaction to a situation where we believe our well-being is endangered or threatened in some way. More specifically, others think of it as being closely associated with fear, and it is maintained that the fear can lead to anger, with the anger becoming guilt and finally if the guilt is not relieved, ending in a state of serious depression. As far as children are concerned, adults can take measures to eliminate or at least minimize fears. When this is achieved anxiety can be relieved. In a later chapter on "Controlling Fears" we will go into detail on how this can be accomplished by adults.

Although the above brief discussion of certain terms does not exhaust the vocabulary used in connection with stress, it is hoped that it will serve in part to help the reader distinguish the use of terms basic to an understanding of the general area of stress. Other terminology will be described as needed at the time we are dealing with certain specific topics.

## WHAT IS THE CONCEPT OF STRESS?

In discussing the stress concept we do not intend to get into a highly technical discourse on the complex and complicated aspect of stress. Nonetheless, there are certain basic understandings that need to be taken into account, and this requires the use of some technical terms. For this reason we are providing a "mini-dictionary" of terms used in the discussion to follow.

**ACTH** — (AdrenoCorticoTropic Hormone) secreted by the pituitary gland. It influences the function of the adrenals and other glands in the body.

**ADRENALIN** — A hormone secreted by the medulla of the adrenal glands.

**ADRENALS** — Two glands in the upper posterior part of the abdomen that produce and secrete hormones. They have two parts, the outer layer, called the *cortex* and the inner core called the *medulla.*

**CORTICOIDS** — Hormones produced by the adrenal cortex, an example of which is *cortisone.*

**ENDOCRINE** — Glands that secrete their hormones into the blood stream.

**HORMONE** — A chemical produced by a gland, secreted into the blood stream, and influencing the function of cells or organs.

**HYPOTHALAMUS** — The primary activator of the autonomic nervous system, it plays a central role in translating neurological stimuli into endocrine processes during stress reactions.

**PITUITARY** — An endocrine gland located at the base of the brain about the size of a pea. It secretes important hormones, one of which is the ACTH hormone.

**THYMUS** — A ductless gland that is considered a part of the endocrine gland system, located behind the upper part of the breast bone.

Although there are various theories of stress, one of the basic and better known ones is that of the previously-mentioned Hans Selye. We have already given Selye's description of stress as the "nonspecific response of the body to any demand made upon it." The physiological processes and the reactions involved in Selye's stress model is identified as the *General Adaptation Syndrome* and consists of the three stages of *alarm reaction, resistance stage,* and the *exhaustion stage.*

In the first stage (alarm reaction), the body reacts to the stressor and causes the hypothalamus to produce a biochemical "messenger," which in turn causes the pituitary gland to secrete ACTH into the blood. This hormone then causes the adrenal gland to discharge adrenalin and other corticoids. This causes shrinkage of the thymus with an influence on heart rate, blood pressure and the like. It is during the alarm stage that the resistance of the body is reduced.

In the second stage, *resistance* develops if the stressor is not too pronounced. Body adaptation develops to fight back the stress or possibly avoid it, and the body begins to repair damage, if any.

The third stage of *exhaustion* occurs if there is a long-continued exposure to the same stressor. The ability of adaptation is eventually exhausted and the signs of the first stage (alarm reaction) reappear. Selye contended that our adaptation resources are limited, and when they become irreversible, the result is death. (The goal of all of us, of course, should be to keep our resistance and capacity for adaptation.)

Although Selye's stress model which places emphasis upon "nonspecific" responses has been widely accepted, in recent years the nonspecific nature of stress has been questioned by some. Findings of such notable scientists as John Mason[1] of Yale University tend to support the idea that there are other hormones involved in stress in addition to those of the pituitary-adrenal system.

As in the case of all scientific research, the search for truth continues and more sophisticated procedures will emerge in the study of stress. Current theories will be more critically appraised, and other theories will be advanced. In the meantime, there is abundant evidence to support the notion that stress in modern society is a serious threat to the well-being of man if not controlled, and of course the most important factor in such control is man himself.

## HOW DO WE REACT TO STRESS?

There are different ways in which reactions to stress can be classified, and in any kind of classification there is likely

---

[1]Mason, John W., et al, "Selectivity of Corticosteroids and Catecholamine Responses to Various Natural Stimuli," *Psychopathology of Human Adaptation*, New York, Ed. George Serban, Plenum Publishing Company, 1976.

to be some overlapping. For our purposes we are using the two broad classifications of *physiological* reactions and *behavioral* reactions.

### Physiological Reactions

1. Rapid beating of the heart, which is sometimes described as "pounding of the heart." We have all experienced this reaction at one time or another as a result of great excitement, or as a result of being afraid.
2. Perspiration, mostly of the palms of the hands, although there may be sweating in some persons at various other parts of the body.
3. The blood pressure rises, which can be referred to as a hidden reaction because a person is not likely to be aware of it.
4. The pupils of the eyes may dilate, and again the person will not necessarily be aware of it.
5. The stomach seems to "knot up," and we sometimes refer to this as "feeling a lump in the pit of the stomach." This of course can have a negative influence on digestion.
6. Sometimes a person experiences difficulty in swallowing and this is often characterized as a "lump in the throat."
7. There may be a "tight" feeling in the chest and when the stressful condition is relieved one may refer to it as "getting a load off my chest."

What these various physiological reactions mean is that the body is gearing up for a response to a stressor. This is called the *fight or flight* response and was first described as an *emergency* reaction by the late Walter Cannon[2] the famous Harvard University Physiologist a good many years ago. The fight or flight response prepares us for action in the same way that it did for prehistoric man when he was confronted with an enemy. His responses were decided on the basis of the particular situation at hand, such as fighting an opponent for food or fleeing from a wild animal that provided him with an overmatched situation.

In modern times with all the potentially stressful conditions

[2]Cannon, Walter B., *The Wisdom of the Body*, New York, W. W. Norton, 1932.

that provoke a fight or flight response, modern man uses these same physiological responses to face up to these same kinds of situations. However, today, we generally do not need to fight physically (although we might feel like it sometimes), or run from wild animals, but our bodies still react with the same fight or flight response. We still need this means of self-preservation occasionally, but not in response to the emotional traumas and anxieties of modern living.

In the case of children this excessive physiological reactivity for the purpose of self-protection is not appropriate in most of the child's world. For children, neither fighting or fleeing is an acceptable response—socially or otherwise. As a result there is no easy way for this internal level of arousal to dissipate except over time. If the situation persists, the child will have difficulty adapting and there is a risk of chronic physiological reactivity being maintained. This is likely to be accompanied by high levels of anxiety. Therefore, it becomes extremely important that adults, in their dealings with children, make every effort to keep it under control.

## Behavioral Reactions

For purposes of this discussion, we will consider *behavior* to mean anything that one does as a result of some sort of stimulation. A person under stress will function with a behavior that is different from ordinary behavior. We will arbitrarily classify these as: (1) *counter* behavior (sometimes referred to as defensive behavior), (2) *dysfunctional* behavior, and (3) *overt* behavior (sometimes referred to as expressive behavior).

In counter behavior a person will sometimes take action that is intended to counteract the stressful condition. An example, is taking a defensive position. That is, a person practicing an "on-the-spot" relaxation technique, but at the same time, being unaware of it. He may take a deep breath and silently "count to ten" before taking action, if any.

Dysfunctional behavior means that a person will react in a manner that demonstrates impaired or abnormal functioning, which results in a lower level of skill performance than he is ordinarily capable of accomplishing. There may be changes in the normal speech patterns, and there may be temporary impairment of the senses, as well as temporary loss of memory. Many of us have experienced this at one time or another due to a stress inducing situation, with a "mental block" causing some degree of frustration while we attempt to get back on the original train of thought.

Overt behavior involves such reactions as distorted facial expressions (tics, twitches and biting the lip). There appears to be a need for the person to move about, and thus, pacing around the room is characteristic of this condition. Incidentally, there is a point of view that suggests that overt behavior in the form of activity is preferable for most persons in most stressful situations, and can be highly effective in reducing threat and distress.

Another form of overt behavior is skin flushing, or blushing. This condition may be noticed in children who have been embarrassed in some way by an adult, either on purpose or accidentally.

## WHAT IS PHYSICAL STRESS?

Physical stress can be concerned with unusual and excessive physical exertion, as well as certain physiological conditions brought about by some kind of stress. It can be divided into two general types, *emergency* stress and *continuing* stress. In emergency stress the previously described physiological reactions take place. That is, when an emergency arises such as a bodily injury, hormones are discharged into the blood stream. This involves increase in heart rate, rise in blood pressure, and dilation of the blood vessels in the muscles to prepare them for immediate use of the energy that is generated.

In continuing stress, the body reaction is more complicated. The physiological involvement is the same, but more and more hormones continue to be produced, the purpose of which is to increase body resistance. In cases where the stress is excessive, as in the case of an extensive third degree burn, a third phase in the form of exhaustion of the adrenal glands can develop, sometimes culminating in fatality.

We have said that physical stress can be concerned with unusual and excessive physical exertion. This can be shown in a general way by performing an experiment involving some more or less mild physical activity. First, try to find your resting pulse. Place your right wrist, palm facing you, in your left hand. Now, bring the index and middle fingers of your left hand around the wrist and press lightly until you feel the beat of your pulse. Next, time this beat for ten seconds and then multiply this figure by six. This will give your resting pulse rate per minute. For example, if you counted 12 beats in ten seconds, your resting pulse will be 72 beats per minute. The next step is to engage in some physical activity. Stand and balance yourself on one foot. Hop up and down on this foot for a period of about 30 seconds, or less if it is too strenuous. Then, take your pulse again in the same manner suggested above. You will find that, as a result of this activity, your pulse will be elevated above your resting pulse. Even with this small amount of physical exertion, the body was adjusting to cope with it, as evidenced by the rise in pulse rate. This was noticeable to you; however, other things such as a slight rise in blood pressure were likely involved and of which you were not aware.

## WHAT IS PSYCHOLOGICAL STRESS?

The main difference between physical stress and psychological stress is that the former involves a real situation, while psychological stress is more concerned with foreseeing or imagining an emergency situation. Just the thought of some threatening event may bring about a body response in the same way as in a real situation. The muscles may tense and the heart rate may increase along with the other previously mentioned physiological reactions. A specific example of psychological stress is seen in what is commonly called "stage fright." Incidentally, it is interesting to note that this type of psychological stress may start when one is a child. For example, our studies of stress inducing factors among children have indicated that "getting up in front of the class" is an incident that causes much concern and worry to a large number of children. It has been our personal experience that this condition also prevails with large numbers of adults.

## HOW IS PERSONALITY CONCERNED WITH STRESS?

Before discussing personality as it pertains to stress, let us comment on our own idea of personality. Ordinarily, personality is often dealt with only in terms of its psychological aspect. We like to think of it in terms of the *total* personality. We view this total personality as consisting of physical, social, emotional and intellectual aspects. This conforms more or less with what is becoming one rather common description of personality—"existence as a person"—and this should be interpreted to mean the *whole* person.

While there might be general agreement that personality can influence the way individuals handle stress, there is much less agreement regarding personality as a causal factor in disease. One specific example of this is the difference in opinion regarding the extent to which certain types of personality are associated with heart disease as a result of stress. A case in point is the position taken by Meyer Friedman and Ray Rosenman.[3] They have designated a Type A behavior and a Type B behavior. A person with Type A behavior tends to be aggressive, ambitious, competitive, and puts pressure on himself in getting things done. An individual with Type B behavior is more easy going, relaxed, and tends not to put pressure on himself. With regard to these two types of behavior, Friedman and Rosenman feel that in the absence of Type A Behavior Pattern, coronary heart disease never occurs before 70 years of age, regardless of the fatty food eaten, the cigarettes smoked, or the lack of exercise, but when this behavior is present, coronary heart disease can easily erupt in one's thirties or forties. Incidentally, in this particular regard it should be noted that some authorities are studying the possibility that the condition of Type A behavior in adults could possibly have its origination in children. In fact some researchers have suggested that much of the socialization in modern American society fosters Type A behavior in children. Moreover, studies show that Type A parents tend to drive their children to achieve and excel in school.

---

[3]Friedman, Meyer and Rosenman, Ray H., *Type A Behavior and Your Heart*, New York, Alfred A. Knopf, Inc., 1974, p. ix.

This can be harmful, even counter productive if the child comes under too much stress.

## WHAT ARE THE SEX DIFFERENCES IN STRESS?

As far as the sex factor is concerned, it is generally felt that with the recent women's movement, more females will continue to become more susceptible to stress. Walter McQuade and Ann Aikan[4] suggest that there are signs that women's vulnerability is increasing as fast as their independence. They contend that a century ago peptic ulcers were a women's ailment by a ratio of seven to three. Then, as frontier rigors were replaced by industrial ones, life got easier for women and harder for men, and, from 1920 to 1940, nine out of ten victims were males. But since midcentury the incidence of ulcers in women is again on the rise.

An interesting point of view is expressed by Marianne Frankenhaeuser[5] of the Experimental Psychology Research Unit of the Swedish Medical Research Council. She believes that women do not have the same readiness as do men in responding to environmental demands by adrenalin release. She does not feel that this response is due to sex, but more so to a behavior pattern that is common to men in Western society.

The second author of this book[6] was the senior researcher on a study of sex individual differences in stress reactivity. She used a "State Measurement Scale" for the purpose of finding out from male and female college students how they generally felt while experiencing a stress response situation.

The study showed that males and females "perceive" different stress reactions. Of greatest disparity between the perceptions of males and females was the emergence of *gastrointestinal sensitivities* (such as upset stomach) exclusively among males and the emer-

[4]McQuade, Walter and Aikan, Ann, *Stress*, New York, E. P. Dutton and Company, Inc., 1974, p. 7.

[5]Frankenhaeuser, Marianne, "Women and Men Said to Differ in Their Response to Stress," *Psychiatric News*, June 18, 1975.

[6]Humphrey, Joy N., and Everly, George S., "Perceived Dimensions of Stress Responsiveness in Male and Female Students," *Health Education*, November/December, 1980.

gence of an *aversive affective sensitivity* (such as feeling "high strung") exclusively among females.

It was impossible to attach any significance to the appearance of a gastrointestinal sensitivity among males and an affective sensitivity among females. However, it was speculated that socio-cultural factors may have been involved. The reason for this is that it may be socially acceptable for males to develop "executive ulcers." Regarding the affective sensitivity, generally speaking, males are ordinarily taught to repress emotions, and many males perceive emotion as a sign of weakness. Similarly, females have been traditionally taught that it is appropriate for them to demonstrate emotion. As this era of changing sex roles progresses it will be interesting to see if perceptions of stress responsiveness change as well. If cultural factors do indeed influence perceptions of responsiveness, one might be willing to speculate that, eventually, there would be a more common perception of stress reactions among males and females.

## WHAT CAUSES STRESS?

A fair question to raise might be: What *doesn't* cause stress? We mention this because most human environments and society as a whole are now seen as stress inducing to some degree. In recent years so many causes of cancer have been identified that many persons have almost come to the conclusion that "everything causes cancer." Perhaps the same could be said of stress. Because it seems to have reached "epidemic" proportions, it is easy to believe that "everything causes stress." For example, the very source of livelihood apparently has become so stress inducing that *occupational stress* is a major area of study.

Stress on the job can be described simply as various degrees of compatibility (or incompatibility) between the individual and his work environment. This is a general description that could be applied to all occupations and professions. According to the United States Bureau of Labor Statistics unhappiness with jobs is affecting an astonishing number of people. It is estimated that probably as many as 25 million persons—over a fourth of the American work force—are not satisfied with their jobs. Because of this, cost to employers can run into billions of dollars annually in absenteeism, reduced output and poor workmanship. Added to this is the fact that job dissatisfaction can be a serious stress inducing factor that can cause various health-related problems.

Stress is encountered in many *home* situations when the family itself is under stress and these kinds of conditions can be devastating to children. In a like manner there are many possible stress inducing factors in the *school*, and of all places, this should be an environment that is free from undesirable stress. A later chapter will go into detail regarding the two environments—home and school—as potential causes of stress.

In the past decade or so a number of researchers have studied certain *life events* as causes of stress. They have attempted to find out what kinds of health problems are associated with various events, normal and abnormal, that occur to people either in the normal course of events or as the result of some sort of misfortune. One of the best known studies is that of T. H. Holmes and R. H. Rahe.[7] Following is a list of their ten most serious life events causing stress.

1. Death of a spouse
2. Divorce
3. Marital separation
4. Jail term
5. Death of close family member
6. Personal injury or illness
7. Marriage
8. Fired at work
9. Marital reconciliation
10. Retirement

These same kinds of studies have been conducted to identify those life events that are most stressful for children. Perhaps the foremost authority in this undertaking is one of our coworkers on

---

[7]Holmes, T. H., and Rahe, R. H., "The Social Adjustment Rating Scale," *Journal of Psychosomatic Research*, 1967, 11: 213–218.

a project on childhood stress, R. Dean Coddington, M.D.,[8] Chief of Child Psychiatry, Louisiana State University Medical School at New Orleans. Following is a list of Dr. Coddington's ten most serious life events causing stress for children.

1. The death of a parent
2. The death of a brother or sister
3. Divorce of parents
4. Marital separation of parents
5. The death of a grandparent
6. Hospitalization of a parent
7. Remarriage of a parent to a step-parent
8. Birth of a brother or sister
9. Hospitalization of a brother or sister
10. Loss of a job by father or mother

Readers can make their own comparison of the life events that are most serious to adults and to children. Both of these lists can provide guidance for those adults, particularly parents, who wish to make a serious attempt to control stress in children.

As important as life events scales are as a means of detecting causes of stress, they are not without their critics. Some specialists feel that rather than life events, a better measure is that which is concerned with day-to-day problems. Prominent in this regard is Richard Lazarus,[9] the distinguished stress researcher at the University of California at Berkeley. He and his associates collected data on a number of populations on what he identifies as daily "hassles." Following is the list of hassles for one of these populations—100 white, middle-class, middle-aged men and women.

1. Concern about weight
2. Health of a family member
3. Rising prices of common goods
4. Home maintenance

---

[8]Coddington, R. Dean, Measuring the Stressfulness of a Child's Environment, *Stress in Childhood*, Ed. James H. Humphrey, New York, AMS Press, Inc., 1984.

[9]Lazarus, Richard S., "Little Hassles Can Be Hazardous to Your Health," *Psychology Today*, July 1981.

5. Too many things to do
6. Misplacing or losing things
7. Yard work or outside maintenance
8. Property, investment, or taxes
9. Crime
10. Physical appearance

Regardless of what one accepts as the best assessment of causes of stress—life events, daily problems, or some sort of combination of both—the main objective of adults who deal with children should be to exert their best efforts in bringing stress under control.

## WHAT ARE THE EFFECTS OF STRESS?

The same line of thought that prompted our comment, "everything causes stress," could be applied with the assertion that, "stress causes everything." For example, Kenneth Pelletier[10] has reported that a tragic consequence is that stress-related psychological and physiological disorders have become the number one social and health problem in the last few years, and, further, that most standard medical textbooks attribute anywhere from 50 to 80 percent of all diseases to stress-related origins. Selye went so far as to say that stress is involved in *all* diseases by indicating that every disease causes a certain amount of stress, since it imposes demands for adaptation upon the body. In turn, stress plays some role in the development of every disease; its effects—for better or for worse—are added to the specific changes characteristic of the disease in question.

Recently we reviewed the literature by various medical authorities and found that among various other conditions, the following in some way could be stress related: coronary heart disease, diabetes, cirrhosis of the liver, high blood pressure, peptic ulcer, migraine headaches, multiple sclerosis, herpes, lung disease, injury due to accidents, mental break down, and even cancer. This is almost to

[10]Pelletier, Kenneth R., *Mind As Healer Mind As Slayer,* New York, Dell Publishing Company, Inc., 1977, p. 7.

say, "You name it; stress causes it!" (Incidentally, in the case of stress and cancer: *cortisol* is secreted in greater quantities in response to stress, leading some scientists to believe that cortisol may retard the liver's detoxification of foreign substances including cancer causing chemicals.)

One of the most recent findings has been that there is evidence linking stress and the body's ability to fight disease. Some studies suggest the possibility of immune-system malfunction under stress by comparing the infection-fighting capability of white blood cells taken from normal and severely stressed individuals. In the case of children this becomes all the more serious because to begin with they have lower resistance to disease than adults.

We have come down hard and presented a dismal outlook regarding the effects of stress. But, this is because we have been directing our discussion to *negative* stress. This raises the question: *Is all stress bad?* Indeed not! In fact, Selye himself identified two types of stress as *eustress* (good stress) and *distress* (bad stress). His classic comment that "stress is the spice of life" sums up the idea that stress can be desirable as well as devastating. The only way one could avoid stress would be never to do anything; however, certain kinds of activities have a beneficial influence in keeping the stress mechanism in good shape.

Certainly, the human body needs to be taxed in order to function well, and it is a well-known physiological fact that muscles will soon atrophy if not subjected to sufficient use. Athletes express a desirable aspect of stress when they talk about the exhilarating feeling of "getting up" for a game, and the feeling of the "juices flowing."

At one time or another almost all of us have experienced "butterflies in the stomach" when faced with a particularly challenging situation. Thus, it is important to understand that stress is a perfectly normal human state and that the body is under various degrees of stress in those conditions which are related to happiness as well as those concerned with sadness.

Although both "good" stress and "bad" stress reactions place specific demands for resources on the body, does this mean that good stress is "safe" and bad stress "dangerous?" Two prominent

psychologists, Israel Posner and Lewis Leitner[11] have some interesting suggestions in this regard. They feel that two psychological
variables, *predictability* and *controllability* play an important role.

It can be reasoned that *predictable* pain and discomfort is less
stressful because under this condition a person is said to be capable
of learning when it is safe to "lower his guard" and relax. Since
periods of impending pain are clearly signaled, the person can
safely relax at times when the warning signal is absent. These
periods of psychological safety seem to insulate individuals from
harmful effects of stress. Obviously, persons receiving unsignaled
pain have no way of knowing when it is safe to relax and thus are
more likely to develop serious health problems as a result of the
chronic psychological stress.

The second psychological variable, *controllability* of environmental stressors, which is closely related to coping behavior, also
plays a major part in determining stress effects. The ability to
control painful events may insulate individuals from experiencing damaging stress effects. However, such coping behavior is
beneficial only if a person is given a feedback signal which
informs him that the coping response was successful in avoiding
an impending stressor. Without the feedback of success, active
coping behavior, as such, may increase stress effects since it calls
upon the energy reserves of the body and leaves it in a state of
chronic stress.

The research on predictability and controllability of stressful
events may help answer why it is that people who seek out stressful and challenging activities do not appear to develop stress
illnesses from this form of stress. In contrast, when essentially
similar body reactivity is produced by "bad" stress, then stress
related illnesses can be the result. Perhaps "good" stress does not
produce illness because typically the events associated with it are
planned in advance (they are predictable) or otherwise scheduled
or integrated (they are controlled) into the individual's life. However,
even activities which are generally considered to be pleasant and

---

[11]Posner, Israel and Leitner, Lewis A., "Eustress vs. Distress: Determination by Predictability and Controllability of the Stressor," *STRESS, The Official Journal of the International Institute
of Stress*, Vol. 2, No. 2, Summer 1981, p. 10–12.

exciting (good stress) can produce illness if the individual is not forewarned or has little control over the events. And, unpleasant events (bad stress) may result in stress related illness because they generally come without warning and cannot be controlled.

Some persons have taken the middle ground on this subject by saying that stress is neither good nor bad, indicating that the effect of stress is not determined by the stress itself but by how it is viewed and handled. That is, we either handle stress properly or we allow it to influence us negatively and thus become victims of undesirable stress.

In closing this chapter, and at the risk of repeating ourselves, we want to stress (no pun) the importance of adults knowing how to control stress themselves so that they may be helpful in controlling it in children.

## CHAPTER 2

# HELPING CHILDREN
# UNDERSTAND THEMSELVES

Children face unending challenges and demands in the process of their development. It is up to adults who deal with children to help them adjust to these challenges and demands.

In recent years there has been increasing sentiment among many young men and women of high school and college age that they have a need to *find* themselves. This should fortify the notion that one of the most important aspects of the "growing up" years is that children develop an understanding of themselves. This can be accomplished to some extent when adults improve upon their own knowledge about growing children. And, perhaps more important, being prepared to use this knowledge with children as they grow and develop. This is the major function of this chapter.

In order to set the stage for the discussions that will follow, it appears appropriate at the outset to give consideration to what can be termed "*self*-concerns that induce stress in children." Our long-time work with children has enabled us to identify many of the factors that concern them and at the same time are stressful for them. The following descriptive list of such factors is intended to alert the reader to these child concerns and to facilitate an understanding of some of the things that need to be done in order to assist children in understanding themselves.

1. **Self concerns associated with the meeting of personal goals.** Stress can result if adults set goals for children that are too difficult for them to accomplish. For example, goals may be much higher than a particular home or school environment will permit children to achieve. On the contrary, when goals are set too low, children may develop the feeling that they are not doing as much for themselves as they should. This aspect of stress is also concerned with the fear

22

that some children have that they will not reach their goals in life. It is interesting to note that this can sometimes happen early in a child's life.

2. **Self concerns that involve self esteem.** This involves the way a child feels about himself or herself. Self-esteem can often be highly related to the fulfillment of certain *ego needs*. Some children may feel that there are not enough opportunities offered in modern society for them to succeed. This is perhaps more true of those children who are in a low socioeconomic environment. It bothers some children, too, that adults do not praise them for what they consider to be a job well done.

3. **Self concerns related to changing values.** It is frustrating for some children if they do not understand the value system imposed upon them by some adults. They may develop the feeling that adults are not inclined to place a value on those factors which children believe are important to them personally at their various stages of growth and development.

4. **Self concerns that center around social standards.** In some cases children get confused with the difference in social standards required at the different levels of development. It is sometimes difficult for them to understand that what was socially acceptable at one age level is not necessarily so at another.

5. **Self concerns involving personal competence and ability.** This might well be the self concern that frustrates children the most. Certainly, lack of confidence in one's ability can be devastating to the morale of a child. Many children are becoming increasingly concerned with their ability, or lack thereof, to cope with problems such as expectations of parents and keeping up with school work.

6. **Self concerns about their own traits and characteristics.** Certainly not the least of concerns among children are those factors which are likely to make them different from the so-called average or normal child. This is concerned with the social need for *mutuality,* which means their wanting to be like their peers. When children deviate radically from others in certain traits and characteristics, it can be a serious stress inducing factor. A specific example is the child who is extremely overweight. Some child psychiatrists feel that they are likely to mature into overweight adults and are more

vulnerable to the emotional stress of being fat than adults. Some studies show that overweight children may get lower grades in school, that in some cases they may be discriminated against by teachers, and that they often have poor social skills.

It should be mentioned that all of the self concerns are not characteristic of all children, particularly because of the individual differences among them. That is, what may be a serious self concern for one child may be a minimal concern for another. Nonetheless these self concerns can serve as guidelines for adults in some of their dealings with children.

## UNDERSTANDING CHILD DEVELOPMENT

**Development** is concerned with changes in the child's ability to function at an increasingly higher level. For example, a stage of development in the infant is from creeping to crawling. This is later followed by the developmental stage of walking when the child moves to an upright position and begins to move over the surface area by putting one foot in front of the other.

There are several major theories of child development and each has its devoted followers. Our position is that there are various aspects of each theory that are useful to adults who have responsibilities for guiding children through the developmental years. It will be our purpose, therefore, to make some generalizations of the various theories in an effort to provide useful information for adults to apply in their dealings with children.

Regardless of the theory or combinations of theories of child development that one believes in, all children are going to experience some sort of undesirable stress at one time or another. Many children may never have to contend with more than the average amount of stress that is caused by the growth and developmental process. However, other children may be encumbered with such serious life event stressors as divorce, hospitalization, death in the family and the like.

In general, it is believed that there are about three classifications of children in terms of their ability to deal with stress. There is one group of children that seems to cope with stress extremely well. They recover soon and are able to incorporate the stressful experience into their everyday life experiences. They have a great deal of confidence in themselves and when they encounter a stressful situation and cope with it successfully, their self confidence tends to increase. Incidentally, these are the children who are associated with adults who deal well with stress.

Another group of children consists of those who can cope with stress to some extent but have to "work at it." They gain more self confidence as they improve their ability to cope. However, they do not seem to have as high a level of successes as those classified as "exceptional copers."

The third level of classification involves those children who have a great deal of difficulty in coping with stress. They have problems struggling with some of the processes of normal growth and development. In addition, they become upset and disorganized by the daily hassles as well as life event stressors. As might be expected, this group of children associates with adults—particularly parents—who also have a difficult time adjusting to certain life situations that bring about stress.

The aim of adults, of course, should be to help all children become successful in their dealings with undesirable stress. With some knowledge of child development, adults should be in a better position to provide environments that will help children cope effectively with stress during their developmental years.

## *Total* Development of the Child

There is a great deal of evidence that indicates that a human being must be considered as a whole and not a collection of parts. This means that a child is a unified individual or what is more popularly known as the *whole* child. Adults should think in terms of working in the direction of total development of children in order to adequately meet their developmental needs.

Total development consists of the sum of all the *physical, social, emotional* and *intellectual* aspects of any individual. Thus, these aspects become the various major *forms* of development. Of course, there are other forms of development but they can be satisfactorily subclassified under the above major forms. For example, *motor* development, which is defined as a progressive change in motor performance, is considered as a broader part of the aspect of *physical* development. In addition, *moral* development, which is concerned with the capacity of the individual to distinguish between standards of right and wrong could be considered as a dimension of the broader aspect of *social* development. This is to say that moral development involving achievement in ability to determine right from wrong is influential in the individual's social behavior.

Total development is "one thing" comprising the various major forms of development. All of these components—physical, social, emotional and intellectual—are highly interrelated and interdependent. All are of importance to well-being. The condition of any one of these forms of development affects other forms to a degree and thus, total development as a whole. When a nervous child stutters or becomes nauseated, a mental state is not necessarily causing a physical symptom. On the contrary, a pressure imposed upon the child causes a series of reactions, which include thought, verbalization, digestive processes, and muscular function. It is not always necessarily that the mind causes the body to become upset; the total organism is upset by a particular situation and reflects its upset in several ways, including disturbance in thought, feeling, and bodily processes. The whole child responds in interaction with the social and physical environment, and as the child is affected by the environment, he or she in turn has an effect upon it.

In the foregoing statements we have attempted to point out rather forcefully that the major forms of development are basic components that make for total development of the child. However, each of these forms of development have certain specific concerns and as such warrant separate discussions. This appears extremely important if one is to understand the place of each form of development as an integral part of total development. The following discussions of the physical, social, emotional and intellectual forms of development as they relate to children should be viewed in this general frame of reference.

### Physical Development

One point of departure in discussing physical development could be to say that "everybody has a body." Some are short, some are tall, some are lean and some are fat. Children come in different sizes, but all of them are born with certain capacities that are influenced by the environment.

It might be said of the child that he "is" his body. It is something he can see. It is his base of operation. The other components of total development — social, emotional and intellectual are somewhat vague as far as the child is concerned. Although these are manifested in various ways, children do not always see them as they do the physical aspect. Consequently, it becomes important that a child be helped early in life to gain some degree of control over his body, or what is known as *basic body control.* The ability to do this, of course will vary from one child to another. It will likely depend upon the status of physical fitness of the child. The broad area of physical fitness can be broken down into certain components, and it is important that children achieve to the best of their ability with these components. Although there is not complete agreement on the identification of these components, the general consensus is that they consist of muscular strength, endurance and power; circulatory-respiratory endurance; agility; speed; flexibility; balance and coordination. (A more detailed account of this subject will be dealt with in a later chapter on "Health and Fitness for Stress.")

### Social Development

Human beings are social beings. They work together for the benefit of society. They have fought together in time of national emergencies in order to preserve the kind of society they believe in, and they play together. While all this may be true, social development is still quite vague and confusing, particularly where children are concerned.

It was a relatively easy matter to identify certain components of physical fitness such as strength, endurance and the like. However, this does not necessarily hold true for components of social fitness. The components of physical fitness are the same for children as for adults. On the other hand, the components of social fitness for children may be different from the components of social fitness for adults. By some adult standards children might be considered as social misfits because certain behavior of children might not be socially acceptable to some adults.

To the chagrin of some adults, young children are unhibited in their social development. In this regard we need to be concerned with social maturity as it pertains to the growing and ever-changing child. This is to say that we need to give consideration to certain characteristics of social maturity and how well they are dealt with at the different stages of child development. Perhaps adults should ask themselves such questions as, Are we helping children to become more self-reliant by giving them independence at the proper time? Are we helping them to be outgoing and interested in others as well as themselves? Are we helping them to know how to satisfy their own needs in a socially desirable way? Are we helping them to develop a wholesome attitude toward themselves and others?

**Emotional Development**

In considering the subject of emotion, we are confronted with the fact that for many years it has been a difficult concept to define, and, in addition, there have been many changing ideas and theories in the study of emotion. It is not the purpose here to attempt to go into any great depth on a subject that has been one of the most intricate undertakings of psychology for many years. However, a few general statements relative to the nature of emotion do appear to be in order.

In the preceding chapter we defined emotion as a response an individual makes when confronted with a situation for which he is unprepared or which he interprets as a possible source of gain or loss for him. As will be seen in a later chapter on "Controlling Emotions," there are pleasant emotions and those that are unpleasant. For example, joy could be considered a pleasant emotional experience while fear would be an unpleasant one. It is interesting to note that a good proportion of the literature is devoted to emotions that are unpleasant. It has been found that in books on psychology much more space is given to such emotional patterns as fear, hate and guilt, than to such pleasant emotions as love, sympathy and contentment.

Generally speaking, the pleasantness or unpleasantness of an emotion seems to be determined by its strength or intensity, by the nature of the situation arousing it, and by the way a child perceives or interprets the situation. The emotions of young children tend to be more intense than those of adults. If adults are not aware of this aspect of child behavior, they will not be likely to understand why a child reacts rather violently to a situation that to them seems somewhat insignificant. The fact that different children will react differently to the same type of situation also should be taken into account. For example, something that might anger one child might have a rather passive influence on another.

**Intellectual Development**

Children possess varying degrees of intelligence, and most fall within a range of what is called "normal" intelligence. In dealing with this form of development we should perhaps give attention to what might be considered as components of intellectual fitness. However, this is difficult to do. Because of the somewhat vague nature of intelligence, it is practically impossible to identify specific components of it. Thus, we need to view intellectual fitness in a somewhat different manner.

For purpose of this discussion, we will consider intellectual fitness from a standpoint of how certain things influence intelligence. If we know this then we might understand better how to contribute to intellectual fitness by improving upon some of these factors. Some of the factors that tend to influence intelligence are (1) health and physical condition, (2) emotional disturbance, (3) certain social and economic factors, and (4) children under stress. When adults have a realization of these factors perhaps they will be more able to deal satisfactorily with children in helping them in their intellectual pursuits.

## Stages of Development

In considering the various developmental stages of children, adults should understand that descriptions of such stages reflect the characteristics of the so-called "average" child. Although children are more alike than they are different, they all differ in at least one or more characteristics—even identical twins. Therefore, the reader is reminded that the traits and characteristics included in the following discussion are suggestive of the behavior of the "normal" child. This implies that if a given child does not conform to these characteristics, it should not be interpreted to mean that he or she is seriously deviating from the norm. In other words, it should be recognized that each child progresses at his own rate and that there is likely to be overlapping from one stage of development to another.

We consider the first stage of development to be that period from birth to fifteen months. This can be designated at the "intake" stage because behavior and growth is characterized by *taking in*. This not only applies to food, but other things such as sound, light and the various forms of total care.

At this stage *separation anxiety* can occur. Since the child is entirely dependent upon the mother or other care giver for needs being met, separation may be seen as being deprived of these important needs. It is at this stage that the child's overseer—ordinarily the parent—should try to maintain a proper balance between meeting the child's needs and "overgratification." Many child development specialists seem to agree that children who experience some stress from separation or from having to wait for a need to be fulfilled, are gaining the opportunity to organize their psychological resources, and adapt to stress. On the contrary, children who do not have this balance may be those who tend to disorganize under stress. They fall into the previously-mentioned third level of classification of children who have a great deal of difficulty coping with stress.

During the stage from about 15 months to three years children are said to develop autonomy. This can be described as "I am what I can do" stage. Autonomy develops because most children can now move about rather easily. The child does not have to rely entirely on a care giver to meet every single need. Autonomy also results from the development of mental processes because the child can think about things and put language into use.

It is during this stage that the process of toilet training can be a major stressor. Children are not always given the needed opportunity to express autonomy during this process. It can be a difficult time for the child because he is ordinarily expected to cooperate with and gain the approval of the principal care giver. If the child cooperates and uses the toilet, approval is forthcoming; however, some autonomy is lost. If he does not cooperate disapproval is likely to result. If this conflict is not resolved satisfactorily some clinical psychologists believe it will emerge during adulthood in the form of highly anxious and compulsive behaviors.

The next stage, from three to five years can be described as "I am what I think I am." Skills of body movement are being used in a more purposeful way. Children develop the ability to day dream and make believe and these are used to manifest some of their behaviors. Pretending allows them to be what they want to be— anything from animals to astronauts. It is possible, however, that resorting to fantasy may result in stress because they may become scared of their own such fantasies.

The range of age levels from five through seven years usually includes children from kindergarten through second grade. During this period the child begins his formal education. In our culture he leaves the home for a part of the day to take his place in a classroom with children of approximately the same age. Not only is he taking an important step toward becoming increasingly more independent and self-reliant, but as he learns he moves from being a highly self-centered individual to becoming a more socialized member of the group.

This stage is usually characterized by a certain lack of motor coordination because the small muscles of the hands and fingers are not as well developed as the large muscles of the arms and legs. Thus, as he starts his formal education the child needs to use large crayons or pencils as one means of expressing himself. His urge to action is expressed through movement since he lives in a movement world so to speak. Children at these age levels thrive on vigorous activity. They develop as they climb, run, jump, hop, skip or keep time to music. An important physical aspect at this stage is that the eyeball is increasing in size and the eye muscles are developing. This factor is an important determinant in the child's readiness to see and read small print, and, thus, it involves a sequence from large print on charts to primer type in preprimers and primers.

Even though he has a relatively short attention span, he is extremely curious about his environment. At this stage adults can capitalize upon the child's urge to learn by providing opportunities for him to gain information from firsthand experiences through the use of the senses. He sees, hears, smells, feels and even tastes in order to learn.

The age range of eight to nine years is the stage that usually marks the time spent in the third and fourth grade. The child now has a wider range of interests and a longer attention span. While strongly individualistic, the child is working more from a position in the group. Organized games should afford opportunities for developing and practicing skills in good leadership and followership as well as body control, strength and endurance. Small muscles are developing, manipulative skills are increasing and muscular coordination is improving. The eyes have developed to a point where the child can, and does read more widely. The child is capable of getting information from books, and is beginning to learn more through vicarious experience. However, experiments carry an impact for learning at this stage by capitalizing upon the child's curiosity. This is the stage in the child's development when skills of communication (listening, speaking, reading and writing) and the number system are needed to deal with situations both in and out of school.

During the ages of ten through twelve most children complete fifth and sixth grades. This is a period of transition for most as they go from childhood into the preadolescent period in their development. They may show concern over bodily changes and are some times self-conscious about appearance. At this stage children tend to differ widely in physical maturation and emotional stability. Greater deviations in development can be noted within the sex groups than between them. Rate of physical growth can be rapid, sometimes showing itself in poor posture and restlessness. Some of the more highly organized team games such as softball, modified soccer and the like help furnish the keen and wholesome competition desired by children in this stage of development. It is essential that adults recognize that, at this stage, prestige among peers is more important than adult approval. During this stage the child is ready for a higher level of intellectual skills which involve reasoning, discerning fact from opinion, noting cause-and-effect relationships, drawing conclusions and using various references to locate and compare the validity of information. The child is beginning to show more proficiency in expressing himself through oral and written communication.

Thus, after the child enters school and completes the elementary school years he develops: (1) socially, from a self-centered individual to a participating member of a group; (2) emotionally, to a higher degree of self-control; (3) physically, from childhood to the brink of adolescence; and (4) intellectually, from learning by firsthand experiences to learning from more technical and specialized resources.

## MEETING THE NEEDS OF CHILDREN

In the preceding chapter we mentioned that the main difference between physical stress and psychological stress is that the former involves a real situation, while psychological stress is more concerned with foreseeing or imagining an emergency situation. Many child psychologists believe that undesirable stress is due primarily to the failure of adults to help children meet their needs.

In discussing needs of children it is important that we consider their *interests* as well. Although needs and interests of children are closely related and highly interdependent, there are certain important differences that need to be taken into account.

Needs of children, particularly those of an individual nature, are likely to be innate. On the other hand, interests may be acquired as products of the environment. It is possible that a child may demonstrate an interest in a certain unsafe practice that is obviously not in accord with his needs at a certain age level. The two-year old may be interested in running into the street but this practice might result in injury. Acquiring a particular interest because of environmental conditions is further illustrated in the case of children coming from families that are superstitious about certain kinds of foods or certain foods eaten in combination. In such cases acquiring such an interest from other family members might build up a lifetime resistance to a certain kind of food that might be very nutritious and beneficial to the child's physical needs.

One of the most important aspects is that of obtaining a proper balance between needs and interests. However, arriving at a suitable ratio between needs and interests is not an easy task. Although we should undoubtedly think first in terms of meeting the child's needs we must also have his interest. A general principle by which we might be guided is that the *lower* the age level of children the more we should take the responsibility for meeting their needs. This is based on the obvious assumption that the younger the child the less experience he had had, and, consequently, there is less opportunity to develop certain interests. In other words, a lack of interest at an early age level might possibly be synonymous with ignorance.

### Classification of Needs

It is a well-known fact that children's needs have been classified in many ways. However, it should be borne in mind that any classification of human needs is usually an arbitrary one made for a specific purpose. For example, when one speaks of biological needs and psychological needs it should be understood that each of these, although classified separately, are interdependent. The classification of needs used here is the same that we used for the forms of development. That is, physical, social, emotional and intellectual needs.

#### Physical Needs

Needs of a physical nature are concerned with the basic anatomical structure and basic physiological function of the human organism. Included here, of course, are the need for food, rest and activity, and proper care of the eyes, ears, teeth and the like. Physical needs are also concerned with such factors as strength, endurance, agility, flexibility and balance that we previously considered as elements of physical fitness of the human organism. It is interesting to note that the physical aspect can be measured most accurately with objective instruments. We can tell how tall or heavy a child is at any stage of development. Moreover, persons trained for the purpose can derive accurate information with measurements of blood pressure, blood counts, urinalysis and the like.

## Social Needs

The importance of social needs is brought more clearly into focus when we consider that most of what human beings do, they do together. Social maturity, and, hence, social fitness, might well be expressed in terms of fulfillment of certain needs. In other words, if certain social needs are being adequately met, the child should be in a better position to realize social fitness. Among other needs, we must give consideration to (1) the need for *affection* which involves acceptance and approval by persons; (2) the need for *belonging* which involves acceptance and approval of the group; and (3) the need for *mutuality* which involves cooperation, mutual helpfulness and group loyalty.

When it comes to evaluating social outcomes we do not have the same kind of objective instruments that are available in computing accurately the physical attributes of children. In some cases, and primarily for diagnostic purposes, in their dealings with children, some school systems have successfully used some of the acceptable *sociometric* techniques. However, at best the social aspect is difficult to appraise objectively because of its somewhat vague nature.

## Emotional Needs

In dealing with emotional needs we repeat what we said earlier that we are confronted with the fact that for many years there have been many changing ideas and theories as far as the study of emotion is concerned. The degree to which emotional needs are met has considerable influence upon the development of the child's personality and upon mental health. Among the basic emotional needs are: (1) the need for a sense of security and trust; (2) the need for self-identity and self-respect; (3) the need for success, achievement and recognition; and (4) the need for independence.

The human personality is remarkably adaptive and some children whose basic emotional needs are not met in one way or another are sometimes able to compensate in ways which still make for satisfactory mental health. For example, some orphan children learn to develop certain of their personality resources and thereby compensate for having received what in most people would be considered a lack of security. Still, the fact remains that beyond a certain point, if these emotional needs are not met, the child can easily develop emotional problems or personality disorders.

It is currently believed by many psychiatrists and psychologists that the foundation of mental health problems are laid in early childhood. Thus it appears that adults play a major role in the development of "good" or "poor" mental health. Clearly, the obligations of adults and particularly of parents are great in this matter of providing the home conditions which will encourage the forming of the basis of good mental health in the years to come. It is obvious that all children cannot intellectualize upon or evaluate their basic emotional needs. Most children react instinctively in seeking to meet their needs; thus many facets of their personality and patterns of adjustment are being developed unconsciously. It is for this reason that most people do not know how they got many of their strong feelings about such things as jealousy, hostility, sex, religion and the like. At any rate how children see themselves, other people of both sexes, and the world at large, and how they interpret and react to each of these, is molded and colored by their early experience.

When we attempt to evaluate the emotional aspect we tend to encounter much the same situation as when we attempt to assess the social aspect, and the emotional aspect might well be more difficult to appraise than the social aspect. Among some of the methods used by researchers to attempt to measure emotional response are blood pressure, blood sugar analysis, pulse rate and galvanic skin response (a device somewhat like the lie detector apparatus). These methods and others that have been used by investigators of human emotion have various, and perhaps limited degrees of validity. In attempting to assess emotional reactivity, investigators sometimes encounter problems in determining the extent to which they are dealing with a purely physiological response or a purely emotional response. Then, too, the type of emotional pattern is not identified by the measuring device. For example, a *joy* response and an *anger* response could show the same or nearly the same measure in microamperes when using a galvanic skin response device.

## Intellectual Needs

Satisfactorily meeting children's intellectual needs is one of our greatest concerns as it is of paramount importance to success in school and life in general. There appears to be rather general agreement as to the intellectual needs of children. Among others, some of these needs include: (1) a need for challenging experiences at their own level; (2) a need for intellectually successful and satisfying experiences; (3) a need for the opportunity to solve problems; and (4) a need for opportunity to participate in creative experiences instead of always having to conform.

Assessment of the intellectual aspect is made by a variety of IQ tests. However, this measurement should not always be used as a valid measure of a child's intellectual ability, and many child psychologists tend to feel that this is more a measure of achievement than it is of basic intelligence. Incidentally, two of our associates on a child stress project Bernard Brown and Lilian Rosenbaum[1] of Georgetown University have discovered that children who are under stress score 13 percent lower on intelligence tests than children who are not.

It can be concluded that when adults have a better realization of the physical, social, emotional and intellectual need of children, perhaps they can deal more satisfactorily with children in helping them with their life pursuits and to cope with undesirable psychological stress.

## TOWARD A CHILD'S UNDERSTANDING OF *SELF*

Among the various other struggles a child encounters in the process of growing and developing is that of gaining an understanding of *self*. It is the purpose of this section of the chapter to provide information that will help adults become more successful in their efforts to aid children in the process of self-realization.

It should be recalled that at the outset of this chapter a comment was made about young men and women being concerned

---

[1]Brown, Bernard and Rosenbaum, Lilian, *Stress Effects on IQ* Paper presented at the American Association for the Advancement of Science, Detroit, Michigan, 1983.

with finding themselves. We believe that if adults can assist children throughout the growing years to gain a better understanding of themselves, it will become an easier matter for them to move into young adulthood.

Insofar as possible, thoughtful adults, and particularly parents, should provide an environment that is a stable sanctuary which the child knows will be there when needed. Children need to be accepted for themselves, with their own unique abilities and limitations. They need to be permitted to grow and learn at their own rate and in their own way—and not be made to feel inadequate in growing and learning even though they may not conform themselves to some standard or "norm." They need to identify as a distinct individual; and their uniqueness is deserving of respect. As children mature they should have the opportunity to assume independence and responsibilities that are commensurate with their age and abilities.

Children require control and discipline which is consistent, reasonable, and understandable to them. A few clear and simple rules are usually entirely adequate and tend to give children a feeling of security in that they know what they can do and what they cannot do. Therefore, it may be said that children need defined limits to prevent them from destructive behavior and perhaps from even destroying themselves. It is important to emphasize that consistency in all aspects of the environment is very important. For example, acts for which they are ignored, praised, or punished should not vary from time to time. If they do, children are likely to become confused and their adjustments made more difficult. Similarly, expression of love should not be spasmodic; nor should the threat of withdrawal of love be used as an occasional weapon to control behavior.

Modern standard dictionaries ordinarily list almost 500 hyphenated words beginning with *self*—from *self*-abandonment to *self* worth. In this discussion we are going to be concerned primarily with *self*-image, or how one conceives oneself or one's role. Reflecting back to our comments on physical development it should be recalled that it was suggested that as far as the child is concerned, *he is his body;* that is, he is essentially concerned with his *physical self.* It is something he can see and is much more meaningful to him than his social, emotional and intellectual *self.* This being the case we now turn our attention to what we call *body-image* which is the child's picture of his bodily person and his abilities. It has been clearly demonstrated that when adults help children improve upon body-image then a basic understanding of the broader aspect of self will more likely be established.

### Determining Deficiencies in Body-Image

One of the first steps is to attempt to determine if a child has problems with body-image. In this regard it is doubtful that there is any absolutely foolproof method of detecting problems of body-image in children. The reason for this is that many mannerisms said to be indicative of body-image problems can also be the same as for other deficiencies. Nevertheless, those persons who are likely to deal in some way with children should be alert to certain possible deficiencies.

Generally speaking, there are two ways in which deficiencies concerned with body-image can be detected, at least in part, by observing certain behaviors. And, second, there are some relatively simple diagnostic techniques which can be used to determine such deficiencies. The following generalized list contains examples of both of these possibilities and is submitted to assist the reader in this particular regard.

1. One technique often used to diagnose possible problems of body-image is to have children make a drawing of themselves. The primary reason reason for this is to see if certain parts of the body are *not* included in the drawing. The personal experience of one of the present authors as a Certified Binet Intelligence Test Examiner revealed possibilities for such a diagnosis in the test item involving *picture completion.* In this test item a partial drawing of a "man" is provided for the child to complete. Since the child's interest in drawing a man dates from his earliest attempts to represent things symbolically, it is possible, through typical drawings by young children, to trace certain characteristic stages of perceptual development. It has also been found in recent years that the

procedure of drawing a picture of himself assists in helping to detect if there is a lack of body-image.

2. Sometimes the child with a lack of body-image may manifest tenseness in his movements. At the same time he may be unsure of his movements as he attempts to move the body segments.

3. If the child is instructed to move a body part such as placing one foot forward, he may direct his attention to the body part before making the movement. Or, he may look at another child to observe the movement before he attempts to make the movement himself. This could be due to poor processing of the input (auditory or visual stimulus) provided for the movement.

4. When instructed to use one body part (arm) he may also move the corresponding body part (other arm) when it is not necessary. For example, he may be asked to swing the right arm and he may also start swinging the left arm simultaneously.

5. In such activities as catching an object, the child may turn toward the object when this is not necessary. For example, when a beanbag thrown to him approaches close to the child, he may move forward with either side of the body rather than trying to retrieve the beanbag with his hands while both feet remain stationary.

### Improving Upon Body-Image

In general, it might be said that when a child is given the opportunity to use his body freely in enjoyable movement an increase in body-image occurs. More specifically, there are activities which can be used in helping children identify and understand the use of various body parts as well as the relationship of these parts.

Over a period of years we have conducted a number of experiments in an attempt to determine the effect of participation in certain body-movement activities on body-image. The following is an example of this approach utilizing the game *Busy Bee*.

In this game the children are in pairs facing each other and dispersed around the activity area. One child who is the *caller* is in the center of the area. This child makes calls such as "shoulder-to-shoulder," "toe-to toe," or "hand-to-hand." (In the early stages of the game it might be a good idea for the adult leader to do the calling.) As the calls are made, the paired children go through the appropriate motions with their partners. After a few calls, the caller will shout, "Busy Bee!" This is the signal for every child to get a new partner, including the caller. The child who does not get a partner can name the new caller.

This game has been experimented with in the following manner: As the children played the game, the adult leader made them aware of the location of various parts of the body in order to develop the concept of full body-image. Before the game was played, the children were asked to draw a picture of themselves. Many did not know how to begin, and others omitted some of the major limbs in their drawings. After playing Busy Bee, the children were asked again to draw a picture of themselves. This time they were more successful. All of the drawings had bodies, heads, arms, and legs. Some of them had hands, feet, eyes and ears. A few even had teeth and hair.

Among the following activities will be found those which can be used for diagnosis for lack of body-image, body-image improvement, evaluation of body-image status or various combinations of these factors. Some of the activities are age-old while others have been developed for specific conditions. They can be carried out in various environments such as school, camp or home where other family members can be the players.

**Everybody Goes**

All of the children (except the one who is *It*) line up side by side at one end of the activity area. *It* stands in the middle of the activity area facing the line. At the opposite end of the area there is a goal line. The distance of the playing area can be variable. The game is started with the following rhyme:

Head, shoulders, knees and toes.
Eyes, ears, mouth and nose.
Off and running everybody goes.

On the last word, "goes," the children in the line run to the other end and try to reach the goal line without being tagged by *It*. All of those tagged become helpers for *It* and the game continues with the children running to the opposite end on signal. If the game is played in its entirety, it continues until there is one player left who can be declared the winner.

As the rhyme is recited, the children in the line do the following motions: Head—place both hands on the head; shoulders—place both hands on the shoulders; knees, bend at the waist and place both hands on the knees; toes—bend on down and touch the toes and resume standing position; eyes—point to the eyes; ears—point to the ears; mouth—point to the mouth; nose—point to the nose.

It might be a good idea in the early stages for the adult leader to recite the rhyme. The leader can be the judge of how fast this should be done. The more accomplished the children become, the faster the rhyme can be recited, and the children themselves can recite it in unison. When the game is first played, the leader can observe closely for those children who are reacting by doing what the rhyme says. It may be found that some are having difficulty. Thus, the activity becomes a means for diagnosing a lack of body-image. It will be noticed that with practice children will improve in their response to the rhyme.

### Come With Me

Several children form a circle with one child outside the circle. The child outside the circle walks around it, taps another child and says, "Come with me." The child tapped falls in behind the first child and they continue walking around the circle. The second child taps a child and says, "Come with me." This continues until several children have been tapped. At a given point the first child calls out, "Go home!" On this signal all the children try to get back to their original place in the circle. The first child also tries to get into one of these places. There will be one child left out. He can be the first child for the next game.

In the early stages of this game the adult leader should call out where each child is to be tapped. For example, "on the arm," "on the leg," etc. After a while the child doing the tapping can call out where he is going to tap the child. The leader can observe if children are tapped in the proper place.

**Mirrors**

One child is selected as the leader and stands in front of a line of children. This child goes through a variety of different movements and the children in the line try to do exactly the same thing; that is, they act as mirrors. The leader should be changed frequently.

In this activity the children become aware of different body parts and movements as the child in front makes the various movements. The adult leader should be alert to see how well and how quickly the children are able to do the movements that the child leader makes.

**Move Along**

The children lie on their backs on the floor. The adult leader gives a signal such as the beat of a drum or clap of the hands and the children move their arms and legs in any way they choose. The leader then gives the name of a movement such as "Move your legs like a bicycle," and then gives the signal to begin the movement. If the leader wishes, some sort of scoring system can be devised to reward those children who make the correct movement in the fastest amount of time.

The leader should observe closely to see how rapidly the children respond to the movements called. In addition, the leader should observe to see if some children are waiting to see what others are going to do before making the correct movement.

**Change Circles**

Several circles are drawn on the floor or outdoor activity area with one less circle than the number of participants. The one child who does not have a circle can be *It* and stands in the middle of the area. The adult leader calls out signals in the form of body parts. For example, such calls could include, "hands on knees." "hands on head," "right hand on your left foot," and so on. After a time the leader calls out, "Change circles!" whereupon all the children try to get into a different circle while the child who is *It* tries to find a circle. The child who does not find a circle can be *It* or a new person can be chosen to be *It.*

The leader should observe closely to see how the children react to the calls, and whether or not they are looking at the other children for clues. As time goes on and the children become more familiar with body parts, more complicated calls can be made.

### Body Tag

In this game one child is selected to be *It.* He chases the other children and attempts to tag one of them. If he is successful the child tagged can become *It.* If *It* does not succeed within a reasonable amount of time a new *It* can be selected. In order to be officially tagged, a specific part of the body must be tagged by *It.* Thus, the game could be shoulder tag, arm tag, or leg tag as desired.

The leader observes the child to see whether or not he tags the correct body part. To add more interest to the activity, the leader can call out the part of the body to be tagged during each session of the game.

The above activities consist of just a few possibilities for use in improving upon body-image and, thus, an understanding of self. Creative adults should be able to think of numerous others that could satisfy this purpose.

CHAPTER 3

# HELPING CHILDREN
# UNDERSTAND ABOUT STRESS

W hy does my heart beat faster when I get excited? Why do my
hands sweat when I am afraid? Why do I breathe fast when
something makes me mad? Such questions from children tend to
verify the fact that they know that something is going on in their
bodies, although they are not necessarily aware that these conditions could be reactions to stress.

It is well known that the stress concept is complicated and
complex. How, then does an adult attempt to develop such a
complex concept with young children? Certainly, an adult needs
at least a general understanding about stress; the material provided in Chapter 1 can serve as a basis for such information for
adults. It is up to them to convey this as best they can in "children's
language." However, it might be necessary and certainly most
helpful at times for adults to resort to professionally prepared
scientific materials. Therefore, the major thrust of this chapter is
to discuss in detail three of the better known approaches that
have met with success in helping children to understand about
stress. These are: (1) *The Humphrey Program,* (2) *Kiddie QR,* and
(3) *Tiger Juice.*

## THE HUMPHREY PROGRAM

Our good friend, the late Hans Selye, was extremely influential
in the development of many stress-related innovations. The germ
of the idea for The Humphrey Program actually originated with
Dr. Selye. It came about during some correspondence with him
about how teachers can cope with stress. This correspondence
revealed that a major interest of his was in the area of developing

informational materials that would bring the stress concept down to the level of understanding of young children. In fact, in the introduction to *Helping Children Understand About Stress* (The Humphrey Program) Dr. Selye wrote: "I think it is extremely important to begin teaching the stress concept to children at a very early age, because all codes of behavior sink in best if a tradition is established. There are many books on stress written for adults, but to my knowledge none are really suitable for very young children; and I think this can best be done by putting the basic concepts of my philosophy of life (which is built on purely physiological research) in the form of children's language taking the text from my book *Stress Without Distress*."[1]

The present authors had published a number of children's books and in addition had conducted research in stress-related matters. Therefore it seemed feasible to explore the possibility of preparing learning materials about stress for young children. Consequently, a meeting was arranged with Dr. Selye at the International Institute of Stress in Montreal to formulate plans to proceed with the project. At this conference it was decided that the material would be based on the principal behavioral implications of the code of behavior set forth in Dr. Selye's best-selling book, *Stress Without Distress*.

### Collection of Data

One of the first concerns was to determine how broad the concept of stress would need to be for satisfactory internalization. This necessitated collection of data on stress-related experiences of children; that is, it was important to find out how definitive children would be when considering stressful situations as well as to ascertain their level of understanding about stress. This was accomplished by developing an inquiry instrument that involved a combination of free-response and projective type items. Following are some examples of the items along with some representative responses of children.

---

[1]Humphrey, James H. and Humphrey, Joy N. *Helping Children Understand About Stress,* (Introduction by Hans Selye, p. 5) Long Branch, New Jersey, Kimbo Educational, 1980.

1. How do you feel when you do something nice for someone?
   I feel nice myself and I feel happy.
   I feel good and glad I did it.
   A good feeling comes over my body.
   I feel good and will do it again.
   I feel happy and proud.
2. How do you feel before you take a test in school?
   I get a funny feeling in my stomach.
   I feel shaky or something scary.
   I feel nervous and afraid I am going to fail.
   I feel shaky, nervous and sick.
   I feel like I might sweat or something.
3. How do you feel when you can't do something you want to do?
   I get mad and I don't like it.
   I feel like killing the person who said I couldn't do it.
   I feel like screaming and throwing a fit.
   I feel awful and if I can't do something I want to try to forget about it.
   I feel let down.
4. I feel best when _____
   I do something right.
   I do something I always wanted to do.
   I do something good or make somebody happy.
   someone cares about me.
   when I'm with my friends.
5. I feel worst when _____
   I'm told I did bad.
   report cards come out.
   I've done something wrong.
   I fail.
   I work to do something and don't make it.
6. Sadness is _____
   not feeling good.
   being left out.
   losing your best friend.
   not being able to do what I want to do.
   getting something you like taken away.

7. Happiness is _____
   being loved.
   when I learn something new.
   when school is out.
   when I get things my way.
   getting all my work done.

Data were collected on more than 100 children through this process and as a result sufficient information was provided to help determine the extent of the breadth of stress concepts as well as possibilities of internalization of the concepts. This information was also used in discussion with children to help them understand how and why their bodies responded in various ways during happy and unhappy situations.

## Plan for the Development of Stress Concepts

The next step was the identification of concepts of stress and codes of behavior in *Stress Without Distress* that would be suitable for development with children and that could also be placed in a frame of reference to which they could relate.

With the above information at hand, the next step was to develop a thematic scenario to which children could relate. It was decided that this could best be accomplished by taking a central character (child) through an entire day with supporting characters in the form of parents, peers, a sibling, and a teacher. The environment included the home, school, and play time experiences. A story of approximately 1,500 words was developed in line with this scenario. The application of a standard readability formula placed the reading level of the story at seven years eight months with a two-month measurement error. (A total of 27 picture clues and illustrations that accompany the text tend to reduce the readability level appreciably.)

## Application of the Materials

The next undertaking was to try out the material with a large number of children from six to nine years. Because the reading level was too high for the children in the lower age range, the story was *read to* them. The purpose of the tryout was to determine the extent to which the children could understand the concepts as well as to evaluate their interest in the content.

The tryout was deemed successful, since teachers who observed the children indicated that they displayed considerable interest in the content as compared to other listening and reading materials. Some typical responses of teachers were:

1. "I feel that the story was well written; however, primary children's interest will always dwindle when there are no accompanying illustrations." (As mentioned previously, the story in final form is accompanied by 27 picture clues and illustrations.)
2. "The children maintained an interest throughout the entire story and participated actively in the discussions that followed."
3. "The children seemed to understand and remember the events in the story."

The final step of the project was to have the material reproduced for widespread distribution to individuals who might wish to provide information for young children to help them have a better understanding of stress. To this end the project was produced by Kimbo Educational of Long Branch, New Jersey in 1980 under the title of *Helping Children Understand About Stress*. It consists of a long play recording (listening experience), ten books of the story, *Ted Learns About Stress* (reading experience) and a teacher's manual.

Following is the complete story, *Ted Learns About Stress* (without the illustrations). The reader might wish to experiment with children in the reading of the story. For children who have difficulty with reading, it can be read to them.[2]

## TED LEARNS ABOUT STRESS

Ted was fast asleep.
He seemed to have a smile on his face.

---

[2]Permission to use this material has been granted by Kimbo Educational, Long Branch, New Jersey.

"Come on Ted, time to get up," called his Mother.

All at once Ted sat up in bed.

"Gee, Mom, I was having a nice dream."

"Oh, what were you dreaming about?" asked his Mother.

As Ted got out of bed he said, "I was dreaming about being a helper and it gave me a very good feeling."

Ted's Mother agreed by saying, "I'm sure it was a good feeling. Come on and get dressed so you won't be late for school."

As Ted and his older sister Marie and their Father and Mother were sitting at the breakfast table, Ted's Mother said, "Ted told me he had a dream about being a helper and it gave him a very good feeling."

"I am sure it did," said Ted's Father, "because when we help others we also help ourselves."

"I wish someone would help me with these words," said Marie.

Ted asked, "What kind of words; could I help?"

"I don't think so," said Marie, "Some of these are even too hard for me. Thanks anyhow."

"Marie, what are you supposed to do?" asked her Father.

Marie answered, "Well, you see Dad, our teacher gave us ten words. They are the same but have different meanings. We are to tell two meanings of each word."

Ted asked, "Would you tell me one of the words, Marie?"

"Well," said Marie, "one of the words is stress."

"I don't know that one," said Ted. "Maybe Dad can help you."

His Father smiled and said, "Maybe I can help with that one. In my work as a builder we use the word stress to mean how strong something should be. Then we can tell how strong to build it."

"Oh!" said Ted. "You mean like my bike needs to be strong enough to hold me up."

"That's right Ted," said his Father.

"You know," said Mother, "I read the other day about stress

and our bodies. It can be caused by many things. There are kinds of stress which can be bad for your body."

Ted asked, "How is that, Mom?"

"Well, Ted," replied his Mother, "it seems that when we worry about something it can be bad for us."

"I think I know what you mean," said Ted, "I was worrying the other day about a spelling test. It gave my body a funny feeling."

"In what way, Ted?" asked his Father.

Ted answered, "My heart beat faster and my hands were sweating."

Marie said, "That's the way I feel when I think about these words."

Ted thought for a moment and then said, "There are your two meanings, Marie. Stress when you build something and stress which does something to our bodies."

"Hey, that's great," exclaimed Marie, "thanks for the help."

Mother smiled and said, "Glad we could help."

Looking at Ted she said, "Ted, remember how you felt in your dream about helping? Well, that's the way I feel now."

Her Father smiled at Marie and said, "I feel good about helping too."

All at once some voices from outside called, "T-e-d, are you ready? Come on or we'll be late for school."

"That's Sally and Bob," said Ted as he got up from the table.

Mother gave Ted his books and lunchbox and he said good-bye to his family and went outside to meet his friends.

As the three children walked along they talked about school.

Ted asked, "Are you on Mrs. Davis' Helper Chart today?"

"I am," said Sally, "I'm the board washer this week."

Bob said, "I like that job but I have a different one this week."

Then Ted said, "Mrs. Davis needs good helpers. It's nice when everyone has a job to do."

"I like Mrs. Davis and I like to help her," said Sally.

"We better hurry a little faster," said Bob, "or we'll be late."

Soon they were at school and the first person they saw was Mrs. Davis.

Mrs. Davis smiled and said, "Good morning, you look like you are ready for school today."

"I hope so," said Ted.

Then Mrs. Davis asked, "Do you all remember your jobs for this week?"

Together Sally and Bob answered, "Yes, and we were talking about it on the way to school."

"We like being helpers," said Ted. "It makes it better for everyone."

"I'm glad you feel that way," said Mrs. Davis. "We are going to start our unit on Helping Others today."

Sally, Bob and Ted took their seats in the room along with the other children.

Mrs. Davis said, "We are starting our unit on Helping Others today. If you will tell some ways to help, I will put them on the board. Ted, since you and Sally and Bob were talking about helping, would you like to start?"

Ted said, "Well, you can help your family by working around the house."

"Good!" said Mrs. Davis, "Let's write that down."

"We can help each other by sharing," said Sally.

"Fine, Sally," said Mrs. Davis. "Can you say more about that?"

Sally answered, "We need to take turns at things. Everyone can't be first all the time."

"That's right," said Bob. "When we play a game, everyone should have a chance to be *It*."

"Good, Bob," said Mrs. Davis. "Anything else?"

"Debbie, your hand was up."

"Yes, Mrs. Davis," said Debbie. "When we all share in doing a job, the job is done better."

Mrs. Davis seemed very pleased as she said, "Those are all good ways to help. You have also said why it is important to help."

Mrs. Davis went on, "Now, can we talk a little bit about how it feels to help? Can you say in just one word how it makes you feel to help?"

"It makes me feel good," said Tommy.

"It makes me feel happy," said Dorothy.

"It makes me feel glad," said Bill.

"Very good!" said Mrs. Davis. "We are getting a fine start on our unit on Helping Others. When school is out today I hope you remember the things we talked about."

The rest of the day seemed to pass quickly and before long the bell rang to end the school day.

As Ted, Sally and Bob walked home from school, Ted said, "School was fun today."

"I'll say," said Bob, "I liked it."

"Mrs. Davis is a good teacher," said Sally.

Before long they reached Ted's house. Sally and Bob said good-bye to Ted.

Ted saw his Mother in the yard and called, "Hi, Mom!"

Mother called back, "Hello, Ted how was school today?"

"Great," said Ted. "Everyone liked it because we started our unit on Helping Others."

Ted talked to his Mother for a little while and then thought he would stay outside and play until it was time for dinner.

Soon Ted's Mother was calling him, "Come on Ted, get ready to eat."

Ted got ready for dinner and went to the table with the rest of the family.

It was a time for the family to talk about what they had done during the day.

Mother started by asking Father, "How was your day, Fred?"

He replied, "It was pretty good because we started plans for a new building."

Then Ted said, "You will have to build it strong to hold up."

His Father smiled and said, "Right, Ted, you remember talking about stress at breakfast."

Marie said, "Do you remember that stress was one of my words with more than one meaning?"

Mother asked, "Did you talk about it in school?"

"Yes, and I said that you had read about stress and our bodies."

"Oh!" said Mother. "You mean that some kinds of stress are good and some kinds are bad?"

"That's right," said Marie. "Our class felt that we should learn to deal with stress."

"I agree," said Father. "When you learn how to do that you will enjoy life more."

Mother looked at Ted and asked, "How about your day, Ted?"

Ted smiled happily, "School was fun today. We talked about helping others."

"Well that sure is a good idea," said his Father.

Then Ted said, "Everyone agreed that it was a good feeling to help."

Mother said, "Do you remember that we decided that at breakfast?"

Marie seemed to be thinking about what was being said. She thought out loud, "It all works together. Helping others makes you happy and being happy helps you deal with stress."

"Well, I guess that is what it is all about," said Mother.

"Right!" said Ted. "I hope I have another dream tonight about helping. Then I'll wake up feeling great in the morning."

In summary, because the material for this stress-related story for children was scientifically selected, prepared, and tested, it might well be considered unique in the area of children's listening and reading material. To date, the results have been most satisfactory in terms of children's interest in the listening and reading content as well as their understanding of certain broad concepts of stress—particularly as they relate to the code of behavior in the book *Stress Without Distress*.

## KIDDIE QR

An outstanding innovative approach to helping children understand about stress is the process known at the *Quieting Reflex* (QR). The technique was originated by Charles F. Stroebel, Director of Research, Institute of Living, Hartford, Connecticut, who was a collaborator of ours on one of our own childhood stress projects. At the beginning, this approach was used exclusively with adults. Dr. Stroebel credits his wife Elizabeth and another associate, Dr. Margaret Holland with modifying the technique for use with young children.[3]

Based on a solid foundation of objective evidence, Kiddie QR emphasizes the concept of the goodness of the body and "making friends with one's body." Essentially, it is considered an educational preventative health care program for helping children in the four to nine-year age range deal with stress. The program is divided into 16 *experiential elements* on tapes of three to seven minutes in length. The tapes are accompanied by several booklets which explain in detail how to use the material. As an example, *Element Number* 16, "My very good feeling self," is designed to help a child understand that homeostasis is a state of physiological and psychological equilibrium. It reinforces the concept that the body is inherently good and that with care and the built-in safety mechanisms each child can expect a healthy happy life.

One of the very important dimensions of Kiddie QR is its emphasis on *mind/body integration* as a means of helping children understand about stress and what to do about it. Dr. Stroebel and his associates feel that children and adults alike confuse the common experience in daily life of being "psyched" and "hyped." They interpret the expression "psyched up" as a heightened mental state which may be likened to a positive enthusiastic state of healthy stress (eustress) or simple healthy excitement. The expression "hyped up" implies an excessive degree of body arousal, suggestive of non-productive energy. Because of the pressures of

---

[3]Stroebel, Elizabeth, Stroebel, Charles F., and Holland, Margaret, *Kiddie QR A Choice for Children*, Wethersfield, Connecticut, 1980.

daily living it is easy to confuse these states and assume that both reactions are part of ongoing healthy behavior. For good health and development, it is essential to have access to the full spectrum of our emotional and physical reactions, to be aware of the subleties in states or shifts in arousal level that are natural and that make us wonderfully unique.

In the Kiddie QR approach a fairly simple illustration is used to help children grasp the complex idea of mind/body integration. This is the comparison between the interaction of emotional and physiological reaction in their bodies and the construction and operation of a toy car.

Car Frame . . . . . . . . . . . . . . . . . Bones
Radiator. . . . . . . . . . . . . . . . . . Blood
Carburetor/Exhaust . . . . . . . . . . Lungs
Pumps . . . . . . . . . . . . . . . . . . . Heart
Headlights. . . . . . . . . . . . . . . . . Eyes
Tires. . . . . . . . . . . . . . . . . . . . . Feet
Windows . . . . . . . . . . . . . . . . . Mouth/Breath
Brakes/Power . . . . . . . . . . . . . . Muscles
Gasoline . . . . . . . . . . . . . . . . . Stress Hormones
Battery. . . . . . . . . . . . . . . . . . . Energy Source
Accelerator/Speedometer . . . . . . Emotions

This comparison helps children to conceptualize how the emotional arousal level mechanisms in the brain trigger off physiological reactions within the body.

In order for their toy race car to perform well, they must control the speed, check out the car and the track for problems, and keep an alert mind and calm body to keep the car functioning at optimal performance. A crucial factor is that of balancing moments of lower speed with moments of heightened acceleration through shifting into the appropriate speed gear. Similarly, children learn that their body functions much like the mechanism and operation of a car and that their emotions act as the control center of their body frame, just as the accelerator pedal acts as the speed control in the car. And as in the car race, they recognize that the signaling mechanisms ready the body systems and organs to *gear up* to a higher arousal state when their emotional gas pedal or stress hormones alert their brain to do so and when to *gear down* when their emotions signal the brain to slow down or lower the arousal.

It is felt that it is extremely important to emphasize the healthy aspect of these unique body mechanisms; that is, there are appropriate times to use our passing gear: for playing tag, racing on our bikes, and jumping up and down for joy when we are happy. Passing gear is a body safety feature for emergencies too—when we are late for dinner and want to "step on the gas" so as to run quickly home, or for more serious problems when we need to move away from real danger. Within the discussion children can talk about why it would not usually be appropriate or safe to use our passing gear in the house where we might break something or hurt ourselves, or while we are trying to do our school work and the "wiggle" gear would interfere with mental performance.

One aspect of the approach, "QR and My Body Bike Cycle," is an experiential exercise in shifting body gears through learning to discriminate among the physiologic changes that can be observed and felt. For example, the children can observe changes in their breathing pattern, in feeling their heart rate accelerate as well as experiment with overt muscle tensing. They experiment with arousal states by exploring appropriate and inappropriate "body speeds," by learning how to balance the emotions that accompany stressful situations with comfortable emotions and unstressful situations. In general, they learn that unnecessary wear and tear on the body diminishes performance and creativity. This exercise lends itself nicely to physically show how "hyper" or Type A tendencies are similar to keeping the body in passing gear all the time. The experiential work coupled with discussions is an avenue of communication that makes sense to children and is a way to talk about the consequences of these long-term patterns in a positive non-threatening framework so that the child need not become fearful or feel guilt.

The analogy of the car and the body helps a child visualize mind/body integration. Here is an appropriate place in discussing it with children to talk about how our emotions trigger off uncomfortable body sensations such as butterflies in the stomach, or a pounding heart, or the scary uneasy feelings that we experience without understanding their origins.

All of the *Elements* in the QR program are especially useful for children who display hyperactive behavior tendencies and who need a means to understand their body arousal state which is disquieting to them. By becoming aware of the mind/body integration concept, they can acquire practical skills and ways to discriminate their emotional and physiological speed and then how to adjust their mental and physical arousal levels for the task at hand.

## TIGER JUICE

This interesting approach combines relaxation and desensitization. It was developed by Stewart Bedford the well-known California Clinical Psychologist. The technique derives its name from materials prepared for the purpose by Dr. Bedford.[4]

This children's booklet is illustrated with simple line drawings and is 52 pages in length. Readability level of the book is such that 63 percent of the words are at the first to second grade level; 16 percent of the words are at the third grade level; and six percent of the words are above the fourth grade level. The content of the book and the illustrations portray the evolution of stress reactions; the physiology and function of stress; and simple ways to manage stress through relaxation.

There is a manual for parents and teachers which gives specific instructions for teaching children about stress. In addition, the manual explains the use of relaxation, breathing, biofeedback, diet and exercise. Desensitization is covered by a technique that is called "Relaxed Reruns" which consists of simple imagery exercises teachers and parents can use with children.

Two cassette tapes were developed as part of the material. Side one of the first tape has a reading of the children's booklet with musical notes telling them when to turn the pages. Side two has a guided imagery exercise demonstrating the functioning and physiology of stress. The second tape has progressive relaxation, autogenic training, and meditative procedures for the children

---

[4]Bedford, Stewart, *Tiger Juice, A Book About Stress for Kids (of all ages)*, Chico, California, Scott Publications, 1981.

and for parents and teachers. This tape is the same on both sides.

This technique has met with great success in its use with children at the third and fourth grade levels. It has also been of value with early adolescent "slow readers." In addition, in the case of younger children, the technique has been very successful when the prepared material is presented (read to) children by adults. After a great deal of research with this approach Dr. Bedford has concluded that it is important for adults to learn stress management techniques themselves if they hope to teach the techniques to children. As mentioned at previous times in our discussions, this is a major thrust of *Controlling Stress in Children*.

## CHAPTER 4

# HOME AND SCHOOL CONDITIONS
# THAT CAN CAUSE STRESS

For nine months of the year the home and school environments occupy practically all of the time of children in the age
range from 6 to 12. Specifically, children spend about two-thirds of
their approximately 15 waking hours in the home environment
and the remaining one-third in the school environment. It is the
purpose of this chapter to examine certain aspects of these two
environments that induce stress in children. Such information
should be useful to adults by helping them to become more aware
of these factors and at the same time assisting children to deal with
them.

## HOME STRESS

Reflecting back to the ten most serious life events causing stress
in children presented in Chapter 1, it is interesting to note that
fully 90 percent of these were in some way connected with home
and parents.

Changes in society with consequent changes in conditions in
some homes are likely to make child adjustment a difficult problem.
Such factors as changes in standards of female behavior, larger
percentages of both parents working, economic conditions, mass
media such as television, as well as numerous others can compli-
cate the life of the modern-day child.

Some child psychiatrists are convinced that some home conditions can have an extremely negative influence on the personality
and mental health of some children, not only at their present stage
of growth and development, but in the future as well. In fact,
studies show that the interaction of stress factors is especially

important. Most of these studies tend to identify the following factors to be strongly associated with childhood (and possibly later) psychiatric disorders: (1) severe marital discord, (2) low social status, (3) overcrowding or large family size, (4) paternal criminality, (5) maternal psychiatric disorder, and (6) admission into the care of local authorities.

It is estimated that, with only one of the above conditions present, a child is no more likely to develop psychiatric problems than any other child. However, when two of the conditions occur, the child's psychiatric risk increases fourfold.[1]

In our own extensive surveys, we have found that there were certain actions of parents that induced stress in teachers, and according to the teachers, these parental attitudes might well be considered as stress inducing factors for their students.[2]

Actions of parents that induce stress in teachers can be classified into three areas: (1) lack of concern of parents for their children, (2) parental interference, and (3) lack of parental support for teachers.

In almost half of the cases, lack of parental concern for children was stressful for teachers. They cited such things as parents not caring when a student did poorly, parents not willing to help their children with school work, a lack of home discipline, and stress placed on teachers by the difficult time they had getting parents to conferences.

About a third of the teachers say parental interference was often a result of parents having expectations too high for their children, and this in turn, resulted in parental pressures on children particularly for grades, which may be one of the most serious conditions in schools today—from kindergarten through the university level. In fact, it could be that pressure exerted by parents for grades might be a contributing cause of the increase in the suicide rate among students. Moreover, there are some who believe that par-

---

[1]Rutter, Michael, "Some Group Up Undisturbed: Why?" *The Spectrum*, University of Iowa, Iowa City, Iowa, Winter 1977.

[2]Humphrey, James H., and Humphrey, Joy N., "Factors Which Induce Stress in Teachers," *STRESS*, The Official Journal of the International Institute of Stress, Volume 2, No. 4, Winter 1981.

ents are literally "driving their children to drink" because of an increase in alcohol consumption, possibly due to the "grade pressure syndrome."

The third classification of parental actions causing stress for teachers is that of lack of parental support, and slightly less than one-fourth have identified stress inducing factors here. They were stressed by such factors as not being backed by parents and a general poor attitude of parents toward teachers.

Another important home condition that can induce stress in children is when the family itself is under stress. Parenting itself is an extremely difficult task and the demands of this task are becoming more and more complicated. Consequently, many of the pressures that modern parents are called upon to endure cannot only cause stress for them but can also cause them to induce stress upon their children as well.

It is estimated that one million or more children are abused or neglected by their parents or over "overseers" in our country annually, and that as many as 2,000 die as a result of maltreatment. Authorities suggest that most of this is not caused by inhuman, hateful intent on the part of parents, but rather it is the result of a combination of factors including both the accumulation of stresses on families and unmet needs of parents for support in coping with their child-rearing responsibilities.[3]

## HOME STRESSORS

In Chapter 1 we commented that stress is a state that one is in, and that any stimulus that produces such a state is called a stressor. Thus, simply stated, a home stressor is any situation connected with the home that produces stress.

Several recent studies have addressed the question of multiple stressors in the lives of children by gathering information on a variety of potential home stressors and then determining which of these are most closely linked to adjustment problems. Notable among the researchers in this area are: Dr. Deborah Belle, Direc-

[3]Johnston, Carol A., *Families in Stress,* Department of Health and Human Services, Washington, DC, HHS Publications No. (OHDS) 80-30162, 1979.

tor of the Stress and Families Project at the Harvard University Graduate School of Education and her associate, Dr. Cynthia Longfellow, a Research Fellow on this same project. These researchers prepared a chapter for a volume edited by one of the authors of this book and the discussion that follows summarizes some of the findings derived from this source.[4]

Drs. Longfellow and Belle studied 160 mother-child pairs from low and moderately low-income families in the Boston area. The families were recruited for the study by sending letters home with children from the public schools. There were 82 boys and 78 girls who ranged in age from 6 to 11 years. There was an approximately equal number of working and nonworking mothers. Forty percent of the mothers were single and 60 percent were "coupled"—a term used for women who live with a husband or boyfriend. Approximately 25 percent of the population were Black and 75 percent were White. A three-to-four hour structured interview was conducted with each mother. This interview included questions on demographics, sources of stress across different areas of life, availability of support, feelings of stress and strain, and current mental health status. Mothers were also asked about any physical, emotional, and learning problems their children might have. Children were administered a half-hour interview that asked among other things, about their relationship with their parents.

The measures of life stressors used included the occurrence of discrete life events such as divorce or hospitalization and the existence of chronic life conditions—ongoing characteristics of the family's life which were known or believed to be stressful to children.

The findings of this study showed that a number of everyday life stressors and certain life events were related to the number of behavioral, learning, and emotional problems among school-aged children. Children's adjustment was related to stressors in a variety of areas including mother's mental health, physical health, work situation, social networks (the degree to which a mother's network of friends and relatives had problems that cause her to

[4]Longfellow, Cynthia and Belle, Deborah, Stressful Environments and Their Impact on Children, *Stress in Childhood,* Ed. James H. Humphrey, New York, AMS Press, Inc. 1984.

worry), financial situation, and family characteristics. Those stressors relating to mother's mental health and those relating to other environmental conditions indicated that both types of stressors significantly predicted children's adjustment problems. Children's self-reported happiness in the parent-child relationship was not related to any of the individual stressors except for the stress single mothers experienced over being single. While individual stressors were not predictive of children's happiness, the combined stressors relating to maternal physical and emotional health were predictive of a less happy relationship between parent and child. Thus, the mother's lack of emotional and physical well-being emerged as a type of stressor of central importance to the children.

Observations of children and their mothers found that women who experience more depressive symptoms were less responsive, less nurturing, and more punitive to their young children. Since a supportive relationship between parent and child has been identified as an important buffer between stress and the child's maladjustment, the emotional well-being of mothers plays a critical role in a child's healthy development and adjustment.

It came as somewhat of a surprise to the researchers to find that most of the stressors relating to the mother's marital status and the quality of the marital relationship were not related to children's adjustment or their happiness in the parent-child relationship. For example, neither divorce nor living with a single parent mother was predictive of children's adjustment to happiness. Although many researchers have documented the profound negative impact on children of a conflicted marriage, this study found only a marginally significant association between marital strain and behavioral problems. These researchers' measure of the quality of the marital relationship reflected the mother's degree of satisfaction with the relationship more than the amount of tension or lack of warmth in the relationship—dimensions which have been identified as being particularly stressful for children, and this may account for the difference.

It was interesting that the presence of a "stepfather" may signify a number of other stressors that the child has had to contend with, specifically the loss of a father, adjustment to a new parental figure in the home, and conflicting loyalties between "new" fathers and "old" fathers. Several studies suggest that the school-aged child is particularly vulnerable to a parent's remarriage because he or she is old enough to understand that relationship between parent and child have a permanence beyond time and place. In contrast, preschool children often accept the new stepparent as one of the family since their view of families is more concretely tied to the physical presence of who lives together.

Other stressors that were related to children's adjustment problems included hospitalization and serious accidents or illnesses (the latter only marginally so). It was not clear whether these events contribute to children's adjustment problems or are themselves consequences of stress.

Some have argued that stress causes an increased physical vulnerability among children resulting in a higher rate of accidents. However, this study indicated that neither serious accidents nor hospitalization were consistently related to other life stressors, suggesting that they may be a distinct source of stress for children.

It is interesting to note that maternal employment appeared to benefit both mother and child; that is, employed women were generally less depressed than nonemployed women and their children also had fewer behavioral problems. Not just any job, though, contributes to the well-being of mothers and children. Rather, the quality of that employment is crucial. It was found that children's behavior problems were associated with the level of job stressors reported by their mothers. These stressors included the unavailability of the mother while she was at work, the inflexibility of her schedule for attention to child-related matters, and the lack of paid vacation time.

Family income and money-related problems were both related to children's adjustment, but annual per capita income had no additional effect on children once other sources of stress were accounted for. Thus, low income affects children's well-being by contributing to a stressful environment. Although low income increases the risk of exposure to one or more stressful life conditions, these findings show that low-income children were no more vulnerable to the impact of the sum total of stressors than were the moderately low-income children. In other words, there was no "buffering effect" of higher income, at least not in the low- to moderately low-income families.

There did appear to be a somewhat increased vulnerability among boys to the impact of stressors. While boys and girls differ in their responses to life stressors, boys in particular appear more likely to respond to stress with behavioral, as opposed to neurotic problems.

These researchers emphasize that it is important to view children's reactions to stress in the context of their families. While it was found that a clearcut pattern of negative effects of stressors on children, particularly those stressors relating to maternal well-being, it is suggested that conspicuous life events and conditions explain even less of the variance in outcomes for children than they do for adults. In part this may reflect the fact that the study was originally designed to assess the impact of stressors on maternal mental health and therefore, the interview was geared towards measuring those events and conditions believed to be most stressful to mothers. More likely, though, is the fact that school-aged children are buffered from the impact of life stressors in a variety of ways. Most important is the physical and emotional status of their mothers, but other factors, not included in the analysis are also significant, such as the supportiveness of the relationship between parent and child, the child's social network outside the family, and the child's particular coping strategies. Consequently, we will be better able to guage the impact of stress on children once we know the social and psychological context in which life stressors occur.

## SCHOOL STRESS

There are a number of conditions existing in most school situations that can cause much stress for children. These conditions prevail at all levels—possibly in different ways—from the time a child enters school until graduation from college.

It is possible that some children begin school under stress. Possibly older childhood friends, siblings and even some unthinking parents admonish them with "wait until you get to school—you're going to get it." This kind of negative attitude is likely to increase any "separation anxiety" that the child already has. Learning to cope with the stress of separation can be a very important aspect in the life of some preschool children. For example, Louis Chandler[5] asserts that adults should be alert to the signs of stress and seek to lessen the impact. Compromises should be worked out, not to remove the stress, but to help the child gradually build his tolerance to separation. Understanding, sympathy, and consistent realistic encouragement of independence are needed.

The child's reactions typically may include: temper tantrums, crying, screaming and downright refusal to go; or, in some cases, suspiciously sudden aches and pains which might serve to keep the "sick" child at home. What the child is reacting against is not the school but the separation from the mother. The stress associated with this event may be seen by the child as a devastating loss equated with being abandoned. The child's behavior in dealing with that stress is so extreme as to demand special treatment on the part of the significant adults in his life.

The aim in such cases should always be to ease the transition into school. The school might encourage the mother to remain in the classroom for awhile to help the child adjust. The child might be allowed to bring from home a toy or favored object. This helps the child to maintain a sense of continuity with the home and, like the security blanket, it is a source of comfort. It might also be possible to arrange a visit by the teacher to the child in his home. Finally, it is important to keep in mind that separation is a two-way street. Assuring the parents of the competency of the school staff and of the physical safety of their child may go a long way toward helping lessen the stress. All concerned adults should agree on the goal of returning the child to the normal situation *as quickly as possible*. If there is agreement between parents and school, and a logical plan to carry out the agreement, the effect of separation anxiety can be minimized. "As quickly as possible" in this situation may mean taking a few days or weeks as a transition period. During this period the stress of increased separation can be gradually introduced. If adults act responsibly and with consistency the child will make an adequate adjustment to this daily

---

[5]Chandler, Louis A., *Children Under Stress*, Springfield, Illinois, Charles C Thomas, Publisher. 1982. p. 26.

separation from the family, and, in the process, learn an important lesson in meeting reality demands.

## STRESS AND THE CHILD IN THE EDUCATIVE PROCESS

School anxiety as a child stressor is a phenomenon with which
educators, particularly teachers and counselors, frequently find
themselves confronted in dealing with children. Various theories
have been advanced to explain this phenomenon and relate it to
other character traits and emotional dispositions. Literature on
the subject reveals the following characteristics of anxiety as a
stress inducing factor in the educative process.

1. Anxiety is considered a learnable reaction that has the prop-
   erties of a response, a cue of danger, and a drive.
2. Anxiety is internalized fear aroused by the memory of painful past experiences associated with punishment for the grati-
   fication of an impulse.
3. Anxiety in the classroom interferes with learning, and whatever can be done to reduce it should serve as a spur to
   learning.
4. Test anxiety is a near-universal experience, expecially in
   this country, which is a test-giving and test-conscious culture.
5. Evidence from clinical studies points clearly and consistently
   to the disruptive and distracting power of anxiety effects
   over most kinds of thinking.

It would seem that causes of anxiety change with age as do
perceptions of stressful situations. Care should be taken in assessing
the total life space of the child—background, home life, school
life, age, and sex—in order to minimize the anxiety experienced
in the school. It seems obvious that school anxiety, although
manifested in the school environment, may often be caused by
unrelated factors outside the school.

## TEACHER BEHAVIORS
## THAT INDUCE STRESS IN CHILDREN

In the literature much emphasis has been placed on those factors that induce stress in teachers. It certainly seems appropriate to examine behaviors of teachers that tend to induce stress in their students. The major reason for this, of course, is that teacher behaviors could possibly have a serious negative effect on those they teach. This is not a recent concern because many years ago, on the basis of minimum incidence statistics and pupil-teacher ratios, it was estimated that anxiety may affect as many as two hundred thousand teachers and that through them five million students may be affected.

Equally important, if teachers induce stress in students, the students, in turn, are likely to manifest behaviors that become stress inducing factors for teachers, and thus, the *vicious circle* is allowed to perpetuate.

Perhaps one of the most satisfactory ways of identifying teacher behaviors that are likely to cause stress among students is to simply ask students themselves. In this regard, we conducted a study with fifth and sixth grade children.[6] One question raised with some 200 fifth and sixth grade boys and girls was "What is the one thing that worries you most in school?" As might be expected, there was a wide variety of responses. Nevertheless, the one general characteristic that tended to emerge was the emphasis that teachers placed on competition in so many school situations. Although students did not state this specifically, the nature of their responses clearly seemed to be along these general lines.

Certainly there are many conditions in the school situation that, if not carefully controlled, can cause *competitive stress*. This condition has been described as occurring when a child feels that he will not be able to respond adequately to the performance demands of competition. When the child feels this way, he experiences considerable threat to self-esteem that results in stress.

---

[6]Humphrey, Joy N., and Humphrey, James H., "Incidents in the School Environment Which Induce Stress in Upper Elementary School Children," College Park, Maryland, 1977.

Moreover, competitive stress is a negative emotion that a child experiences when he perceives the competition to be personally threatening.

Whenever possible, teachers might try to guard against those conditions which may result in competitive stress and at the same time emphasize those kinds of conditions which will more likely promote *cooperation*. In this regard, it is interesting to note that the terms *cooperation* and *competition* are antonymous; therefore, the reconciliation of children's competitive needs and cooperative needs is not an easy matter. In a sense, we are confronted with an ambivalent condition that, if not handled carefully, could place children in a state of conflict. Modern society rewards not only one kind of behavior (cooperation) but also its direct opposite (competition). Perhaps more often than not our cultural demands sanction these rewards without provision of clearcut standards of value in regard to specific conditions under which these forms of behavior might well be practiced. Thus, the child is placed in somewhat of a quandary about when to compete and when to cooperate.

In generalizing on the basis of the available evidence with regard to the subject of competition, it seems justifiable to formulate the following concepts.

1. Very young children are not very competitive but become more competitive as they grow older.
2. There is a wide variety in competition among children; that is, some are violently competitive, while others are mildly competitive, and still others are not competitive at all.
3. Boys tend to be more competitive than girls.
4. Competition should be adjusted so that there is not a preponderant number of winners over losers.
5. Competition and rivalry produce results in effort and speed of accomplishment.

## SUBJECT ANXIETY AS A STRESS INDUCING FACTOR

There are various subject areas that could be considered as perenial nemeses for many students. In fact, if you ask an elementary school pupil what he likes best in school the invariable traditional response has been, "recess and lunch." Of course, neither of these are "bone fide subjects" and many pupils when pressed will respond with what they "hate the least."

Probably any subject could be a stress inducing factor for certain students. Prominent among those subjects that have a reputation for being more stress inducing than others are those concerned with the basic *3R'S.* For example, it has been reported that for many children attending school daily and performing poorly is a source of considerable and prolonged stress. If the children overreact to environmental stresses in terms of increased muscle tension, this may interfere easily with the fluid muscular movement required in handwriting tasks, decreasing their performance and further increasing environmental stresses. Most educators have seen children squeeze their pencils tightly, press hard on their paper, purse their lips, and tighten their bodies, using an inordinate amount of energy and concentration to write while performing at a very low level.

Reading is another area of school activity that is loaded with anxiety, stress, and frustration for many children. In fact, one of the levels of reading recognized by reading specialists is called the "frustration level." In behavioral observation terms this can be described as the level in which children evidence distracting tension, excessive or erratic body movements, nervousness and distractibility. This frustration level is said to be a sign of emotional tension or stress with breakdowns in fluency and a significant increase in reading errors.[7]

The subject that appears to stress the greatest majority of students is mathematics. This condition prevails from the study of arithmetic upon entering school through the required courses in mathematics in college. This has become such a problem in recent years that there is now an area of study called "Math Anxiety" that is receiving increasing attention. Prominent among those studying this phenomenon is Sheila Tobias,[8] some of whose thoughts

---

[7]Carter, John L. and Russel, Harold, Use of Biofeedback Relaxation Procedures with Learning Disabled Children, Ed., James H. Humphrey, New York, AMS Press, Inc. 1984.

[8]Tobias, Sheila, "Stress in the Math Classroom," *Learning,* January 1981.

on the matter are summarized in the following discussion.

There appears to be what could be called "math-anxious" and "math-avoiding" people who tend not to trust their problem-solving abilities and who experience a high level of stress when asked to use them. Even though these people are not necessarily "mathematically ignorant," they tend to feel that they are, simply because they cannot focus on the problem at hand or because they are unable to remember the appropriate formula. Thus, a feeling of frustration and incompetence are likely to make them reluctant to deal with mathematics in their daily lives. (And certainly there are innumerable cases where they are almost required to do so.) It is suggested that at the root of this self-doubt is a fear of making mistakes and appearing stupid in front of others.

People carry with them very distinct memories of their first encounters with mathematics, and most of these memories are very likely to be school related. Indeed, long after they have left the classroom some people still experience stress and discomfort when confronting mathematics.

It is believed that there are at least three sources of anxiety commonly found in traditional mathematics classes: (1) time pressure, (2) humiliation, and (3) emphasis on one right answer.

As far as *time pressure* is concerned, such things as flash cards, timed tests and competition in which the object is to finish first, are among the first experiences that can make lasting negative impressions on many young mathematics learners. (The reader should recall that negative aspects of competitive stress were discussed previously.) Speed becomes all important and slower learners are likely to soon become apprehensive when asked to perform a mathematics problem.

One of the strongest memories of math-anxious adults is the feeling of *humiliation* when being called upon to perform in front of the class. The child may be asked to go to the chalkboard to struggle over a problem until the solution is found. If an error is made the child may be prodded to locate and correct it. In this kind of stressful situation it is not surprising that the child is likely to experience "math block," which adds to his sense of humiliation and failure. This should not be interpreted to mean that the chalkboard should not be used creatively to demonstrate problem-solving abilities. A child who successfully performs a mathematical task in front of classmates can have the enjoyable experience of instructing others. Also the rest of the class can gain useful information from watching how another solves a problem. When using chalkboard practice, however, it is important to remember that children profit from demonstrating their competence and not their weaknesses.

Although mathematics problems do, in most cases, have *right* answers, it can be a mistake to focus our attention only on accuracy. In putting too much emphasis on the end product, oftentimes overlooked is the valuable information about the process involved in arriving at that product. It would be well for teachers to reward creative thinking as well as correct answers. Again the reader should not interpret this to mean that the right answer is not important. However, when it is emphasized to the exclusion of all other information, students can become fearful of making mistakes and possibly angry with themselves when they do.

Teachers who make an effort to reduce the number of stressful situations in mathematics programs will not only be helping their students to become better mathematics learners but at the same time they will also be helping them as future adults to be more confident and capable performers in mathematics tasks.

### Preparing Preschool Children for School Mathematics

Since mathematics is such a potential stress inducing factor for children it seems important to provide information which can help to alleviate this condition for the child before he enters school. The following discussion is oriented in this direction.

### Mathematics Readiness

Mathematics readiness means that children should progress through certain developmental stages before they can be expected to be successful in the area of mathematics. For example, a child is probably not ready to take on the task of addition if he has to count to get a sum. Likewise, if he must add to find the product of two numbers, he is not yet ready for multiplication. Therefore, it seems that for the child to achieve mathematics readiness, time should be allowed for maturation of mental abilities and stimulation through experience. It might be said that *experience* is the key to the degree of mathematics readiness a child has attained upon entering school. In fact, research consistently shows that experience is a very important factor in readiness for learning in mathematics.

**What Can Parents Do?**

It should be obvious that most of the child's experience will be the result of efforts of parents and others (siblings and relatives) in the home situation. Because of experiences in mathematics—or lack thereof—children entering first grade vary a great deal in the amount of mathematical learnings they bring with them. It is becoming a more common practice in many schools for teachers to try to determine how *ready* children are to deal with mathematics as they begin first grade. This gives the teacher an idea of the needs of the children, and consequently serves as a basis for the teacher to group children with regard to instruction.

To give the preschool parent some idea of how a teacher might proceed, several *diagnostic* items in the area of mathematics are presented here. It should be clearly understood that these are not standard procedures, but merely representative examples of what teachers might do to help them determine how well acquainted the children are with some of the mathematical experiences that will be dealt with as they begin their formal education. The reason for providing this information is to give the parents of preschoolers an opportunity to see just what might be expected of a child in terms of mathematical understandings upon entering school. When parents have such information, they can provide experiences for children that will improve upon their mathematics readiness.

Ordinarily, these diagnostic items are administered orally with small groups of children. The teacher will try to observe certain behavior responses of children such as hesitation in answering, inattention, lack of ability in following directions, or anything that could be interpreted as immature thinking.

Generally speaking, teachers are concerned specifically with such features as counting, number symbols, number order, ordinal use of numbers, understanding of the simple fraction of one-half, and recognition of coins.

**Counting.** A teacher might try to diagnose ability in counting by having children respond to such questions as: Can anyone count to find how many girls there are in our class? Can anyone count to find how many windows are in our room? Can anyone tell us how many chairs we have? Can anyone tell us how many pictures we have in our room? The teacher observes those children who volunteer and how correct their responses are. Different children are given an opportunity to answer the questions, and each time the responses are observed by the teacher.

**Number Symbols.** In the area of number symbols a teacher might use a procedure like the following: Ten cards with each card having a number (1–10) are placed on the chalkboard tray. The teacher then asks questions such as: Who can find the card that tells us how many ears we have? What is the number? Who can find the card that tells us how many arms we have? What is the number? Which card tells us how many fingers we have on one hand? What is the number? Which card tells us how many doors there are in our room? What is the number?

**Number Order.** In checking children for their knowledge of number order, the same procedure as above is followed except that the card numbers are out of order. Such questions as the following may be asked: Can you help me put these cards back in order? Another procedure used is to ask questions such as: What number comes right after 3? Right after 4? Right after 6? What is the number that comes right before 7? Right before 10? Right before 5? What is the number that comes between 1 and 3? between 6 and 8?

**Ordinal Use of Numbers.** Ordinal numbers are used to show order or succession such as first, second and so on. This can be diagnosed by placing number cards from 1 to 6 in order along the chalkboard tray. The teacher may ask: Who can tell me which is the first card? the third card? the fifth card?

**Concept of One-Half.** To help to determine how well the children understand the concept of one-half, the teacher can use six equal sized glasses. One glass can be full, one can be empty, and the rest of the glasses can be one-fourth full, one-third full, and three-fourths full. Such questions as the following can be asked:

Who can tell which glass is full? Who can tell which glass is empty? Who can tell which glass is half full? Who can tell if there is a glass that is less than one-half full? Can you find a glass that is more than one-half full?

**Coins.** In diagnosing children's knowledge about coins the teacher will probably have ten pennies, one nickel and one dime. The teacher holds up each of the coins to see if the children can identify them. Such questions as the following might be asked: Does a penny buy less than a nickel? Does a dime buy more than a nickel? Which buys more, a penny or a dime? Would you give a nickel for four pennies? Would you give a dime for eight pennies?

With the above information at hand the creative parent should be able to provide experiences that can help the preschooler get ready for school mathematics and thus, perhaps relieve the child of a great deal of stress from "math anxiety" that otherwise could prevail.

The average home situation abounds with many possibilities for mathematics learning experiences. For example, think what could be done in a four-member family just at the dinner table: "Daddy will be late for dinner; how many of us will there be when he gets here?" "John, you drank one-half of your milk; how much do you have left?" *And on and on and on!*

## TEST ANXIETY AS A STRESS INDUCING FACTOR

A few years ago the Society for Research in Child Development released two monographs that contained extensive longitudinal studies on test anxiety as it relates to school children.[9]

The first study represented a limited attempt to determine the relation over time between anxiety and indices of intellectual and academic performance. The following three major results were revealed.

1. The expected negative correlation between test anxiety and IQ tends to be small and insignificant in the first year, but increases significantly in the negative direction over time.

---

[9]Hill, K. T., and Sarasen, S. B., The Relation of Tests Anxiety and Defensiveness to Test and School Performance Over the Elementary School Years. Monograph of the Society of Research in Child Development, 1966, 31 (2 Serial No. 104).

2. These tendencies are more marked and significant when measures designed to correct for sources of distortion of self-report are used.
3. The strength of the negative correlations between test anxiety and IQ scores are consistently stronger when third grade rather than first grade test anxiety scores are used as the predictor variable.

The second study is the summation of a longitudinal study of defensiveness to intelligence and achievement test performance and of school progress over the elementary school years. Some of the major findings indicated the following.

1. There was an increasingly negative relationship between anxiety and test performance over the entire elementary school experience.
2. Anxiety was greater on verbal than on nonverbal tests.
3. Unfamiliar tests aroused much anxiety.

In addition to the above reports, a great deal of research has appeared on test anxiety in various sources over the years. One literature review on the subject suggests the following generalizations.[10]

1. A critical factor is what the test situation means to a particular individual in terms of his learned patterns of response to anxiety. If the test is considered important to the individual and if he is anxious when taking tests, he is more likely to perform poorly on tests than one who is less anxious.
2. There is a negative relationship between level of ability and level of anxiety. Poorer students tend to be most anxious when facing a test.
3. There is a positive correlation between level of anxiety and level of aspiration. Those who are least anxious when facing a test tend to be those who have the least need or desire to do well in it.
4. Extreme degrees of anxiety are likely to interfere with test performance; however, mild degrees of anxiety facilitates test performance.

---

[10]Kirkland. M. C., "The Effect of Tension on Students and Schools," *Review of Educational Research*, 1971, 41.

5. The more familiar a student is with tests of a particular type, the less likely he is to suffer extreme anxiety.
6. Test anxiety can enhance learning if it is distributed at a relatively low level throughout a course of instruction rather than being concentrated at a relatively high level just prior to and during a test.
7. There are low to moderate negative relationships between measures of anxiety and performance on very complex tasks. This negative relationship tends to increase as the task becomes more test-like.
8. Test anxiety increases with grade level and appears to be long range rather than transitory.

What then does the nature of test anxiety imply for educational goals and practice? Perhaps there should be a continuing opportunity for all school personnel and parents to report on their experiences with the tests that have been used. This feedback should also place a great deal of emphasis on the students' reactions to their testing experience. It is essential that the reactions of children that give evidence to emotional disturbance in relation to tests be carefully considered, especially when test results are interpreted and used for instructional, guidance and administrative purposes.

### Helping Children Cope with Test Anxiety

Adults, particularly parents and teachers, can be of assistance to children in the rigors of test-taking. Various recommendations have been made with reference as to how this can be accomplished. One qualified expert, Barbara Kuczen,[11] Professor of Early Childhood Education at Chicago State University, believes that the following suggestions can relieve pressure from the testing scene.

1. Explain the purpose of tests, and make it clear that the child's best is expected, but no more. In this way the child can prepare and relax going into the test, knowing that maximum effort is being expended.

---

[11]Kuczen, Barbara, *Childhood Stress Don't Let Your Child be a Victim,* New York, Delacorte Press, 1982, p. 194-195.

2. When it is known that a test is scheduled, the child should get a good night's sleep, eat a well-balanced breakfast, be dressed in comfortable clothes and leave home in a relaxed, unrushed state.

3. When a test paper is returned, immediately go over the answers and analyze errors. Clear up any misunderstanding about directions, terms or answers so the child will be better prepared next time.

4. Give the child experience working under rigid time limits. Play some games in which the child is timed or allowed a designated number of minutes for completing a task.

5. Advise the child not to get "hung up" on a difficult question, but instead to skip it and do it later, if there is time.

6. Have the child learn to pace the work by looking over the material to see how much needs to be done.

7. Have the child practice reading a question in one place and recording the answer on a separate sheet of paper.

8. Adults should not magnify the importance of tests by getting overexcited by good, or poor, scores. Let the child know that the learning that occurs in school is the prime concern. Test results should reflect that learning.

9. Help the child understand that some test stress can motivate a student to study and achieve. However, if stress is extreme, it can cripple the learner. Work on using ways to relax. (Many of these techniques are presented in Chapters 8 and 9.)

10. Help the child understand that test stress caused by not studying is likely to be inevitable and unacceptable.

It is important to take a positive attitude when considering test results. That is, emphasis should be placed on the number of answers that were correct. For example, the child will be more encouraged if you say, "You got seven right," rather than, "You missed three." There is evidence to show that this approach can help to minimize stress in future test-taking.

## HOW THE SCHOOL LEARNING ENVIRONMENT
## CAN INDUCE STRESS IN BOYS

In general, emotional stress seems to have a greater effect on boys than on girls in both the school and home environment. One possible exception to this in the school situation is that girls are prone to suffer more anxiety over report cards than are boys. Most studies show that boys are much more likely to be stressed by family discord and disruption than are girls, although there does not seem to be a completely satisfactory explanation for this.

In any event, it is interesting to note that many people have been critical of the early school learning environment, particularly as far as boys are concerned. Some of these critics have gone so far as to say that young boys are being discriminated against in their early school years. Let us examine the premise.

A generally accepted description of the term *learning* is that it involves some sort of change in behavior. Many learning theorists maintain that behavior is a product of heredity and environment. Unquestionably, it is very apparent that environment plays a major role in determining one's behavior, and some tend to feel that man is, indeed, controlled by his environment. Nevertheless, we must remember that it is an environment largely of his own making. The issue here is whether or not an environment is provided that is best suited for boys at the early age levels, and further whether such an environment is likely to cause more stress among young boys than young girls.

While the school has no control ancestry, it can, within certain limitations, exercise some degree of control over the kind of environment in which the learner must function. Generally speaking, it is doubtful that all schools have provided an environment that is most conducive to learning as far as young boys are concerned. Many child development specialists have characterized the environment at the primary level of education as *feminized.*

A major factor to consider is that which concerns the biological differences between boys and girls in this particular age range, and it is questionable whether educational planning has always taken these important differences into account. Over the years there has been an accumulation of evidence on this general subject appearing in the literature on child development, some of which will be summarized here.

Due to certain hormonal conditions, boys tend to be more aggressive, restless, and impatient. In addition, the male has more rugged bone structure, and as a consequence greater strength than the female at all ages. Because of this, males tend to display greater muscular reactivity that in turn expresses itself in a stronger tendency toward restlessness and vigorous overt activity. This condition is concerned with the greater oxygen consumption required to fulfill the male's need for increased energy production. The male organism might be compared to an engine that operates at higher levels of speed and intensity than the less energetic female organism.

Another factor to take into account is the difference in Basal Metabolic Rate (BMR) in young boys and girls. The BMR is indicative of the speed at which body fuel is changed into energy, as well as how fast this energy is used. The BMR can be measured in terms of calories per meter of body surface with a calorie representing a unit measure of heat energy in food. It has been found that, on average, BMR rises from birth to about three years of age and then starts to decline until the ages of approximately 20 to 24. The BMR is higher for boys than for girls, particularly at the early age levels. Because of the higher BMR, boys in turn will have a higher amount of energy to expend. Because of differences in sex hormonal conditions and BMR, it appears logical to assume that these factors will influence the male in his behavior patterns.

From a growth and development point of view, while at birth the female is from one-half to one centimeter less in length than the male and around 300 grams less in weight, she is actually a much better developed organism. It is estimated on the average that at the time of entrance into school, the female is usually six to twelve months more physically mature than the male. As a result, girls may be likely to learn earlier how to perform tasks of manual dexterity such as buttoning their clothing. In one of our observational studies of preschool children, we found that little girls were able to perform the task of tying their shoe laces at a rate of almost four times that of little boys.

Although all schools should not be categorized in the same manner, many of them have been captured by the dead hand of tradition and ordinarily provide an environment that places emphasis upon factors such as neatness, orderliness, and passiveness which is easier for girls to conform to than boys. Of course, this may be partly because our culture has forced females to be identified with many of these characteristics.

The authoritarian and sedentary classroom atmosphere that prevails in some schools that involves the "sit still and listen" syndrome, fails to take into account the greater activity drive and physical aggressiveness of boys. What have been characterized as feminization traits prevailing in many elementary schools tend to have an adverse influence on the young male child as far as learning is concerned.

Some studies have shown that as far as hyperactivity is concerned, boys may outnumber girls by a ratio of as much as nine to one. This may be one of the reasons why teachers generally tend to rate young males as being so much more aggressive than females, with the result that young boys are considered to be more negative and extroverted. Because of these characteristics, boys generally have poorer relationships with their teachers than do girls, and in the area of behavior problems and discipline in the age range from five to eight years, boys account for twice as many disturbances as girls. The importance of this factor is borne out when it is considered that good teacher-pupil relationships tend to raise the achievement levels of both sexes.

Various studies have shown that girls generally receive higher grades than boys although boys may achieve as well as and in some instances better than girls. It is also clearly evident that boys in the early years fail twice as often as girls even when there is no significant difference between intelligence and achievement test scores of both sexes. This suggests that even though both sexes have the same intellectual tools, there are other factors that militate against learning as far as boys are concerned.

If one is willing to accept the research findings and observational evidence appearing in the child development literature regarding the premise outlined here, the the question is: What attempts, if any, are being made to improve the condition? At one time it was thought that the solution might lie in defeminization of the schools at the early age levels by putting more men into classrooms. This apparently has met with little success because the learning environment remains essentially the same regardless of the sex of the teacher. Some educators have suggested that little boys start school later or that little girls start earlier. This problem with this, of course, is that state laws concerned with school entrance are likely to distinguish only in terms of age and not sex. In a few remote instances some schools have experimented with separating boys and girls at the early grade levels. In some cases this form of grouping has resulted in both groups achieving at a higher level than when the sexes were in classes together.

The major question that must be posed is: What can be done to at least partially restructure an environment that will be more favorable to the learning of young boys? One step in this direction, recommended by various child development specialists, is to develop curriculum content that is more *action* oriented, thus taking into account the basic need for motor activity involved in human learning. This is to say that deep consideration might well be given to learning activities through which excess energy, especially of boys, can be utilized. The extent to which this kind of curriculum content would make learning less stressful for boys is not entirely known; however, experimentation by the present authors shows definite possibilities along these lines. (NOTE: For a detailed account of this approach the reader is referred to: Humphrey, James H., and Humphrey, Joy N., *Help Your Child Learn the 3R's Through Active Play*, Charles C Thomas, 1980).

Several causes and contributing causes of home and school stress have been dealt with in the preceding discussions. It is possible to eliminate many of the stress inducing factors. For those that cannot be eliminated entirely, serious attempts should be made to at least keep them under control.

# CHAPTER 5

# HEALTH AND FITNESS FOR STRESS

Basic to the control of stress is the attention individuals pay to their own person health and fitness. There are two general factors to consider with regard to stress and health. First, objective evidence continues to accumulate to support the idea that prolonged stressful conditions can be detrimental to the health of some individuals. Second, along with modern techniques of controlling stress are many traditional health practices that long have enabled people to gain greater control over anxieties and help eliminate stressful living. It is the primary function of this chapter to deal with the second factor in the anticipation that the discussion will have a positive impact upon eliminating, or at least minimizing the first factor. We intend to provide information to help adults carry out their own health and fitness program, as well as how they can provide for such programs for children.

In discussing the subject of caring for one's health, we like to deal with what we call the "fitness triangle": (1) nutrition and diet, (2) physical activity and exercise, and (3) sleep and rest. It will be our purpose to deal with these areas in general and how they are concerned specifically with stress.

## NUTRITION AND DIET

It should be obvious that the areas of nutrition and diet are highly interrelated and interdependent. However, there are certain differences that need to be taken into account, particularly as far as the meaning of these two areas are concerned.

## Nutrition

Nutrition can be described as the sum of the processes by which a person takes in and utilizes food substances; that is, the nourishment of the body by food. These processes consist of ingestion, digestion, absorption and assimilation.

*Ingestion* derives from the Latin word "ingestus" meaning to take in, and in this context, it means taking in food, or the act of eating. The process of *digestion* involves the breaking down and conversion of food into substances that can be *absorbed* through the lining of the intestinal tract and into the blood and used by the body. *Assimilation* is concerned with the incorporation or conversion of nutrients into *protoplasm*, which is the essential material making up living cells.

The body needs many essential nutrients or foods to keep it functioning properly. These nutrients fall into the broad groups of proteins, carbohydrates, fats, vitamins, and minerals. Although water is not a nutrient in the strictest sense of the word, it must be included, for nutrition cannot take place without it.

Three major functions of nutrients are building and repair of all body tissues, regulation of all body functions, and providing fuel for the body's energy needs. Although all of the nutrients can do their best work when they are in combination with other nutrients, each still has its own vital role to play.

### Digestion

The digestive system of the body is more than 30 feet long from beginning to end, and the chemical processes that occur within the walls of this mucus-lined hollow tube are extremely complex in nature. From the moment that food is taken into the mouth until waste products are excreted, the body's chemical laboratory is at work. The principal parts of this system are the alimentary canal, consisting of the oral cavity, pharnyx, esophagus, stomach, small intestine, and large intestine. Two additional organs are necessary to complete the digestive system. These are the liver and the pancreas both of which connect to the small intestine. It is from these two organs that many of the essential digestive juices are secreted.

As mentioned previously, the function of the digestive system is to change the composition of foods which we ingest. Reduced to simpler chemical substances, the food can be readily absorbed through the lining of the intestines for distribution by the circulatory system to the millions of body cells. These end products of digestion are in the form of simple sugars, fatty acids, amino acids, minerals, and vitamins.

Digestion is also accomplished by mechanical action. First, the food is broken down by the grinding action of the teeth. This increases tremendously the food surface area upon which the various digestive juices can act. It is then swallowed and eventually is moved through the alimentary canal by a process called peristalsis. This is a series of muscular contractions, which mix the contents of the digestive tract and keep it on the move.

The digestive tract is exceedingly responsive to one's emotional state. Food eaten under happy conditions tends to be readily digested. On the contrary, digestion may be impeded and even stopped for a considerable period of time (as much as a day or more) if severe emotional stress occurs. Extensive nerve connections in the digestive tract tend to make its organs especially susceptible to disorders caused by stress. Examples of some of these disorders are nausea, diarrhea, and colitis (inflamation of the large bowel). In such disorders the organs involved may not necessarily be diseased and there may only be an impaired functioning of the organ. However, many authorities agree that prolonged emotional stress can lead to serious diseases of the digestive tract.

There is a popular belief that a bowel movement per day is essential to health. Moreover, so common rumor has it, to be really effective, this movement should occur at a particular time each day. "Autointoxication" or self-poisoning, it is sometimes claimed, may otherwise result. As a matter of fact, many people do find a bowel movement once a day satisfactory and having it at a particular time, convenient. However, just as some require more than one elimination per day, others find every other day a natural rhythm—and not a cause of constipation (difficult bowel evacuation—a condition that has Americans spending about a half billion dollars annually on laxatives). Thus, the problem is not one of conforming to an arbitrary standard, but discovering one's own natural rhythm and responding to the urge when it comes.

Various things commonly interrupt individual rhythm. For example, altering one's customary routine, rising at a different hour, failing to exercise, and failing to eat enough food containing roughage which normally stimulates peristaltic action. The resulting feeling of discomfort headache, or irritability — "constipation symptoms" — do not necessarily result from self-poisoning or auto-intoxication caused by fecal matter re-entering the blood stream. It seems likely that the emphasis that many parents put on "moving the bowels" leads many people to overexaggerate the importance of failing to do so on schedule. Generally speaking, we are inclined to believe that the individual who has a good diet, including adequate fluids, and is active can trust his body in this as in other regards to tend to itself in its automatic function. Presupposing a generally healthful pattern of living, perhaps patience rather than grim concern and laxatives is the reasonable prescription. Needless to say, a physician should be consulted in the event of marked or prolonged deviation from one's normal bowel-moving behavior.

### Diet

The term *diet* is an all inclusive one used to refer to foods and liquids regularly consumed. The question often raised is: What constitutes a balanced diet? This means essentially, that along with sufficient fluids, one should include foods from the *four basic food groups*. These are the dairy group, the meat group, the vegetable and fruit group, and the bread and cereal group.

A guide to a balanced diet was prepared by the staff of the United States Senate Select Committee on Nutrition and Human Needs. This Committee spent a great deal of time on hearings and research, and some of its recommendations are listed as follows.

1. Eat less meat and more fish and poultry.
2. Replace whole milk with skim milk.

3. Reduce intake of eggs, butter, and other high-cholesterol sources.
4. Cut back on sugars to 15 percent of daily caloric intake.
5. Reduce intake of salt to a total of three grams per day.
6. Eat more fruit, vegetables, and whole grain.

The above recommendations are directed to the general population. However, one important factor must be recommended, and this is that eating is an individual matter. The problem may not be so much one of following an arbitrary diet, but one of learning to know on what foods and proportions of foods one functions best. The body is capable of compensating for an imbalance in nutrients that we fail to get if the shortage is made up within a reasonable period of time. In other words, it is not necessary to have an exactly balanced diet at every meal. Indeed, it is possible to miss meals—even go for several days without food—and show no signs of malnutrition. The important consideration seems to be in the quality of the total intake over periods of time.

The foregoing observations should not be interpreted to mean that you should be indifferent or careless about your food choices. After all, you quite literally are what you eat. It is absurd that some people are more careful about what they feed their pets than they are about what they feed themselves. This kind of thoughtlessness has given rise to the claim that Americans are the most overfed and malnourished people in the world. (Any radical departure from one's diet should be made only under the guidance of a physician and/or a qualified nutritionist.)

## Diet and Stress

With very few exceptions, writers on the subject of stress emphasize the importance of diet as a general health measure. However, the following question arises: Are there any specific forms of diet that can contribute to the prevention of stress and/or help one cope with it?

One specific approach to diet and stress is presented by J. Daniel Palm[1] He suggests that many stress-initiated disorders are related to problems that originate in the regulation of the blood

---

[1]Palm, J. Daniel, *Diet Away Your Stress, Tension & Anxiety*, New York, Doubleday & Company, Inc., 1976.

sugar level. This theory, developed as an extension of the data derived from controlled research, states that an insufficiency of sugar in the blood supplied to the brain is enough of a detrimental condition, and therefore a stress, to initiate physiological responses and behavioral changes that develop into a variety of disorders. A deficiency of blood sugar, which is known to be associated with a variety of disorders, is seen not as a consequence of the disease but a primary and original physiological stress. Behavioral changes may be inadequate or inappropriate attempts of the stress-affected persons to compensate. It is believed that if the stress of an insufficiency of blood sugar can be prevented, various kinds of abnormal behavior can be controlled. To eliminate this stress of a deficiency of blood sugar, Palm proposes a new dietary program. This diet is based on the metabolic characteristics of *fructose* (fruit sugar) and its advantageous use when it is exchanged for glucose or other carbohydrates, which are digested to glucose and then absorbed. (Fructose itself is a normal constituent of sucrose, which is ordinary table sugar; it also occurs naturally in many fruits and constitutes half the content of honey.)

We mentioned previously that you are quite literally what you eat. This old adage has recently been brought more clearly into focus because researchers now know that our bodies synthesize food substances known as *neurotransmitters*. Prominent nutritionists tend to be of the opinion that these neurotransmitters relay messages to the brain which, in turn, affects our moods, sex drive, appetite and even personality. This is to say that adding a certain food or omitting another could be just what a person might need. It is believed that when a person is stressed the body becomes less able to use protein (the protoplasmic matter from which all living animal cells and tissues are formed). Therefore, the general recommendation is that after any kind of stress one should eat more lean meat, fish, or milk products. Also, since stress depletes the supply of Vitamin C and potassium, these should be replaced by eating extra portions of citrus products.

### Vitamins and Stress

From an historical point of view, the realization that vitamins are basic nutrients stands as a milestone in the emergence of the field of nutrition as a scientifically based discipline. Unlike such nutrients as proteins, fats, and minerals, vitamins do not become a part of the structure of the body, but rather they serve as catalysts which make possible various chemical reactions within the body. These reactions have to do with converting food substances into the elements needed for utilization by the various cells of the body. For example, Vitamin D needs to be present if calcium is to be metabolized and made available for use in the blood and bones.

The vitamins with which we are familiar today are commonly classified as *fat* soluble or *water* soluble. This designation means that the one group requires fatty substances and the other water if they are to be dissolved and used by the body. Although a large number of vitamins have been identified as being important to human nutrition, the exact function of many of them has not as yet been determined.

In countries such as the United States it should not be difficult for people to select a diet which is sufficiently varied to include all necessary vitamins. However, poor dietary practices can lead to vitamin inadequacy, and as a precaution many people supplement their diets with vitamin pills. Even though such a supplement may not be needed, when taken in small amounts, the vitamins may do no harm. This is particularly true of the water soluble vitamins in that if one gets more than he needs they will pass right through the body. On the other hand, some of the fat soluble vitamins may be toxic and over doses could render possible harm. Of course, extra vitamins may be prescribed by physicians for a variety of reasons ranging from suspected malnutrition, to pregnancy, chronic fatigue, and postsurgical recovery.

In recent years, a great deal of controversy has emerged as a result of what has been called *megavitamin therapy,* which concerns the use of certain vitamins in massive doses—sometimes as much as 1,000 times the U.S. Recommended Daily Allowances. The proponents for megavitamin therapy believe that massive doses of such vitamins, particularly Vitamin C, and in some cases the B complex vitamins, will prevent certain diseases and very significantly extend life. On the contrary, opponents of the practice maintain that it is not only useless, but in some instances, harmful as well.

It is interesting that there is support in some quarters for massive dosages of certain vitamins as an important factor in surviving stress. In fact, there is a classification of vitamins sold over the counter that are called *stress formula vitamins*, and they go by a variety of brand names. The formula for these is one which includes large amounts of Vitamin C and Vitamin B complex. (Anyone contemplating utilizing a vitamin supplement over and above the U.S. Recommended Daily Allowance might well do so in consultation with a physician and/or qualified nutritionist.)

Practically all theories have enthusiastic proponents as well as equally enthusiastic opponents, and this sometimes results in a great deal of confusion among most of us. The fact that the human organism is so complicated and complex makes any kind of research connected with it extremely difficult. Nevertheless, scholars in the scientific community continue to make important inquiries into the study of human needs. We emphasize again, and forcefully, that individuals concerned in any way with their own specific dietary problems should consult a physician and/or a qualified nutritionist for guidance.

## Eating Habits of Children

Adult supervision, especially that of parents, is of utmost importance in children's eating habits. However, unfortunately in some cases some parents may be the child's worst enemy as far as eating habits are concerned. The nagging parent who tries to ply the child with foods that he may not like and the constant admonishment of "clean your plate" oftentimes can do a great deal of harm to the child's present and future eating habits.

The diets of some families include too much of certain foods that can be potentially harmful to the adult members as well of its children. A case in point is the intake of *cholesterol*. Excessive amounts of this chemical component of animal oils and fats are deposited in blood vessels and may be a factor in the causation of hardening of the arteries leading to a heart attack.

In his interesting book *The Healing Heart*, Norman Cousins[2]

---

[2]Cousins, Norman, *The Healing Heart*, New York, W. W. Norton & Company, 1983, p. 66.

suggests that the accumulation of these fatty substances is not something that begins in upper middle age. On the contrary, the process can begin in early childhood. A 1982–83 study of children in New York City and Los Angeles conducted by Dr. Ernest L. Wynder of the American Heart Foundation, showed average cholesterol levels of 180 for children in the 10–12 year age range. This is about 50 points above normal for children of this age. Continuing on the same course would lead to cholesterol levels close to or above 300 by the age of 35. (Physicians vary in their beliefs about safe levels of cholesterol; however, some use a very broad range of 150–300 as being normal, the average of this range being 225.)

At about the end of the first year of life most children begin to have a rather remarkable change in their eating habits. For one thing, there is likely to be a large decrease in the intake of food. Many parents who do not understand the process of child growth and development worry needlessly about this condition. What actually happens is that after the first year the growth rate of the child declines and as a consequence his need for calories per pound of body weight becomes less. This causes his appetite to decrease and this can vary from one meal to another, sometimes depending upon the kind and amount of activity in which the child engages. Thus, a parent who is aware of this, will not expect the child of two or three years of age to eat the way he did when he was six-months old. This knowledge for the parent is very important because then he or she will not be so concerned with the *quantity* of the child's intake of food. This is to say that parents should be more concerned with *quality* of food than amount of intake.

Sometimes a child may develop a sudden like or dislike for certain foods. Reasons vary for this change in attitude. He may want a particular cereal because of a prize in the box, and then he may turn the food down because he is disenchanted and does not want the prize. Fortunately, more often than not, such likes and dislikes are not long-lasting, and adults should not worry too much about them.

It is a good practice to provide a rather large variety of foods early in the child's life. This helps to prevent a child from forming set opinions on food likes and dislikes. Adults should set an example by not allowing their own dislikes to influence children.

Adults often complain that a particular child is a "poor eater." When this occurs it is important to try to identify the cause of this problem. It may be that the child too frequently eats alone, and is deprived of the pleasant company of others. Or perhaps the portions are too large, particularly if he feels that he must consume all of it. As mentioned elsewhere mealtime should be a happy time. It is not a time for reprimanding and threatening if a child does not eat heartily. Such behavior on the part of adults can place the child under stress and create an eating problem that otherwise would probably not occur.

## PHYSICAL ACTIVITY AND EXERCISE

When used in connection with the human organism, the term "physical" means a concern for the body and its needs. The term "activity" derives from the word "active," one meaning of which is the requirement of action. Thus, when the two words physical and activity are used together, it implies body action. This is a broad term and could include any voluntary and/or involuntary body movement. When such body movement is practiced for the purpose of developing and maintaining physical fitness, it is ordinarily referred to as physical exercise. Our discussions will be concerned with both the broad area of physical activity and the more specific area of physical exercise, and we will take into account how these factors are concerned with all around health as well as how they relate to stress.

### Maintaining a Suitable Level of Physical Fitness

Physical fitness presupposes an adequate intake of good food and an adequate amount of rest and sleep, but beyond these things, activity involving all the big muscles of the body is essential. Just how high a level of physical fitness should be maintained from one stage of life to another is difficult to answer because we must raise the question: Fitness for what? Obviously, the young varsity athlete needs to think of a level of fitness far above that which will concern the average middle-aged individual.

Physical fitness has been described in different ways by different people; however, when all of these descriptions are put together it is likely that they will be characterized more by their similarities than by their differences. For our purposes we will think of physical fitness as the level of ability of the human organism to perform certain physical tasks or, put another way, the fitness to perform various specified tasks requiring muscular effort.

A reasonable question to raise at this point is: Why is a reasonably high level of physical fitness desirable in modern times when there are so many effort-saving devices available that, for many people, strenuous activity is really not necessary anymore? One possible answer to this is that all of us stand at the end of a long line of ancestors, all of whom at least lived long enough to have children because they were fit and vigorous, strong enough to survive in the face of savage beasts and savage men, and able to work hard. Only the fit survived. As a matter of fact, not very far back in your family tree, you would find people who had to be rugged and extremely active in order to live. Vigorous action and physical ruggedness are our biological heritage. Possibly because of the kind of background that we have, our bodies simply function better when we are active.

Most child development specialists agree that vigorous play in childhood is essential for the satisfactory growth of the various organs and systems of the body. It has been said that "play is the business of childhood." To conduct this "business" successfully and happily, the child should be physically fit. Good nutrition, rest, and properly conducted physical activities in school can do much to develop and maintain the physical fitness of children and youth. Continuing this practice throughout life should be an essential goal of all mankind.

The word *exercise* may tend to have strong moralistic overtones. Like so many things that are said to be "good for you," it also tends to give rise to certain feelings of boredom and resentment. Thus, many people draw more than facetious pleasure in repeating old sayings: "When I feel like exercising, I lie down quickly until the feeling goes away," and "I get my exercise serving as pall-bearer for my friends who exercised."

Exercising and maintaining some level of physical fitness makes possible types of meaningful experiences in life that are not otherwise available. These experiences include all manner of physical activity and exercise, including indoor and outdoor sports; and they also include the rich and satisfying interpersonal relationships that are usually associated with these activities. But maintaining some level of physical fitness has still another value that is usually not fully appreciated. This value has to do with the idea that the entire personality of every individual rests upon, and is dependent upon, its physical base. The entire personality—which is to say, all of the intellectual, emotional, and social components—is threatened when the physical component is weak and unreliable. It has been claimed by some fitness enthusiasts that academic performance, emotional control, and social adjustment are improved when an adequate level of physical fitness is improved; and many case histories and clinical data would tend to support this contention. However, at the moment, we are content to argue that a reasonably solid physical base is more likely than a shaky one to serve as a successful launching pad for other personality resources. In other words, children and adults will be likely to do better in everything they undertake if they feel good, their vitality is high, and they are capable of prolonged effort.

## Developing an Activity Program

In recommending physical activity—vigorous pleasurable physical activity—to adults and children, we are doing so not only in the sense that it will be likely to reduce, eliminate, or avoid chronic fatigue and lessen the impact of acute fatigue. We recommend it, too, on the basis that the ability to move the body skillfully in a wide variety of ways, and for appropriate periods of time, is a dimension of human experience that is fundamental, pleasurable, and meaningful. It is part of being human and alive.

The traditional recommendation has been to consult a physician before undertaking a physical activity program. However, a recent publication by the National Heart, Lung, and Blood

Institute[3]—the government agency that finances much of the heart disease research—tends to dispel this notion. The position is taken that failing to exercise regularly can be far more dangerous than by abstaining because one may not be willing to consult a doctor first which may be preventing millions of people from starting an exercise program. Our own position is that it is a personal matter as to whether or not one should consult a physician before making plans to embark on a physical activity program. If a person feels more comfortable by consulting a doctor first, then perhaps he or she should do so. It is likely that a physician will recommend the program without restriction, or if a physical problem is found, he will take steps to correct it—and he may have suggestions for modifying the program to make it more suitable for a particular individual.

The next consideration is that a program be an individual matter and one that fits one's own needs and wishes. In other words, if a person is not happy with the program, it will be unlikely that it will meet with success as far as personal goals are concerned. Each individual will have to determine which particular approach is best for him, specified physical exercises, recreational sports, or a combination of both. There are three important factors to consider when formulating an exercise program: (1) *frequency,* (2) *persistence and adherence,* and (3) *positive reinforcement.*

Once it is decided what the exercise program will consist of, whether prescribed exercises or recreational sports, the next thing is to determine how many times a week to engage in these activities. It is best to avoid the extremes of the "once in a while" or "always without fail" spurts and try to maintain a regular schedule of three to four times a week. It is also a good idea to work out on alternate days—Monday, Wednesday, and Friday, or Tuesday, Thursday, and Saturday. Sunday can then be used as a makeup day. The hour of the day does not necessarily matter. However, it should be remembered, if it has already been decided, that the fitness program is going to be high on a priority list of things to do, it should

---

[3]*Exercise and Your Heart* may be obtained free of charge by writing to the Consumer Information Center, Dept. P, Pueblo, Colorado 81009.

not be difficult to get into the habit of putting regular workouts into a weekly schedule.

Persistence and adherence are as important to any exercise program as the activities or exercises themselves. Much better and more lasting results will be obtained from a program of three or four steady and regular workouts each week than a program where one goes all out every day for a week and then does nothing at all for the following two or three weeks. A maintenance program, once the desired level of fitness has been reached might be less strenuous and/or slightly less frequent.

Psychological research has discovered that a response that is reinforced by some means is more apt to be repeated than one that is not. When this kind of research was first studied, it was thought that the reward of desired behavior and the punishment of undesired behavior created equal and opposite effects. It was quickly discovered that this was not the case. Punishment seems to have a less permanent effect than reward, and punishment may even bring about the opposite results from those intended. Therefore, it is positive reinforcement that we are seeking. Although there seems to be plenty of positive reinforcement built right into a fitness program (looking and feeling better), praise and encouragement should be forthcoming from others. This also works both ways. If some members of a family are attempting to change their fitness condition, by all means encouragement and praise should be offered. Obviously, it should go without saying that criticizing or belittling are the easiest ways to put a damper on, or even wipe out completely, a person's confidence in himself and his enthusiasm for his program.

## Types of Exercises

For discussion here we will consider three types of exercises: (1) *proprioceptive-facilitative*, (2) *isotonic*, and (3) *isometric*.

### Proprioceptive-Facilitative Exercises

These exercises are those that consist of various refined patterns of movement. Important in the performance of these exercises are those factors involved in movement: (1) time, (2) force, (3) space, and (4) flow.

**Time** is concerned with how long it takes to complete a movement. For example, a movement can be slow and deliberate, such as a child attempting to create his own body movement to depict a falling snowflake. On the other hand, a movement might be made with sudden quickness, such as starting to run for a goal on a signal.

**Force** needs to be applied to set the body or one of its segments in motion and to change its speed and/or direction. Thus, force is concerned with how much strength is required for movement. Swinging the arms requires less strength than attempting to propel the body over the surface area with a standing long jump.

In general, there are two factors concerned with *space*. These are the amount of space required to perform a particular movement and the utilization of available space.

All movements involve some degree of rhythm in their performance. Thus, *flow* is the sequence of movement involving rhythmic motion.

The above factors are included in all body movements in various degrees. The extent to which each is used effectively in combination will determine how well the movement is performed. This is a basic essential in the performance of proprioceptive-facilitative exercises. In addition, various combinations of the following features are involved in the performance of this type of exercise.

1. **Muscular power.** Ability to release muscular force in the shortest time. Example: Standing long jump.

2. **Agility.** Speed in changing body position or in changing direction Example: Dodging run.

3. **Speed.** Rapidity with which successive movements of the same kind can be performed. Example: 50-yard dash.

4. **Flexibility.** Range of movement in a joint or a sequence of joints. Example: Touch floor with fingers without bending knees.

5. **Balance.** Ability to maintain position and equilibrium both in movement (dynamic balance) and while stationary (static balance). Examples: Walking on a line or balance beam (dynamic); standing on one foot (static).

6. **Coordination.** Working together of the muscles and organs of

the human body in the performance of a specific task. Example: Throwing or catching an object.

### Isotonic Exercises

These are the type of exercises with which most people are familiar. An isotonic exercise involves the amount of resistance one can overcome during one application of force through the full range of motion in a given joint or joints. An example of this would be picking up a weight and flexing the elbows while lifting the weight to shoulder height.

Isotonics can improve strength to some extent. They are also very useful for increasing and maintaining full range of motion. Such range of motion should be maintained throughout life if possible, although it can decrease with age and with such musculoskeletal disorders as arthritis. This disease can cause shortening of fibrous tissue structures and this is likely to limit the normal range of motion.

Another important feature of isotonic exercise is that it can increase circulatory-respiratory endurance in such activities as running and swimming. Activities such as these have come to be referred to in recent years as *aerobic* exercises. The term aerobic is derived from the Greek word *aero* which means "air." Thus, these kinds of exercise tend to build up intake of air. The purpose is to strengthen the lungs, heart and cardio-vascular system as a whole.

### Isometric Exercises

Although isometrics do not provide much in the way of improvement of normal range of motion and endurance, they are most useful in increasing strength and volume of muscles. In isometrics, the muscle is contracted, but the length of the muscle is generally the same during contraction as during relaxation. The contraction is accomplished by keeping two joints rigid while at the same time contracting the muscle(s) between the joints. A maximum amount of force is applied against a fixed resistance during one all-out effort. An example of this is pushing or pulling against an immovable object. Let us say that if you place your hands against a wall and push with as much force as you can, you have effected the contraction of certain muscles while their length has remained essentially the same.

## Importance of Physical Activity and Exercise in Controlling Stress

The value of physical activity and exercise as a means of controlling stress is well documented by various authorities. As one specific example, Beata Jencks[4] reports that physical and emotional trauma upset balance of body and mind, and that much energy is wasted in muscular tension, bringing on unnecessary tiredness and exhaustion. If stress reactions become habit patterns, then the muscles and tendons shorten and thicken and excessive connective tissue is deposited, causing a general consolidation of tissues. She comments further that excess energy, released by action of the sympathetic nervous system, if not immediately dissipated by muscular action, produces muscular or nervous tension and that this tension should be dissipated by muscular action in the form of exercise.

Various authentic pronouncements have been made that support the idea that *instant* activity can be beneficial. For example, two distinguished psychologists, Reuven Gal and Richard Lazarus[5] report that being engaged in activity—rather than remaining passive—is preferable in most individuals in most stressful situations and can be highly effective in reducing threat and distress. Lazarus[6] has also maintained that a person may alter his or her psychological or physiological stress reactions in a given situation simply by taking action, and this in turn, will affect his or her appraisal of the situation thereby ultimately altering the stress reaction.

## Physical Activity for Children

One of the most important characteristics of life is movement. Whatever else they may involve, practically all of our achieve-

---

[4]Jencks, Beata, *Your Body Biofeedback at Its Best,* Chicago, Nelson Hall, Inc., 1977, pp. 51 and 172.

[5]Gal, Reuven, and Lazarus, Richard S., "The Role of Activity in Anticipating and Confronting Stressful Situations," *Journal of Human Stress,* December 1975.

[6]Lazarus, Richard S., "The Self-Regulation of Emotion," in *Parameters of Emotion,* L. Levy, Ed., New York, Raven Press, 1975.

ments are based on our ability to move. Obviously, the very young child is not a highly intelligent being in the sense of abstract thinking, and he only gradually acquires the ability to deal with symbols and intellectualize his experience in the course of his development. On the other hand, children are creatures of movement. Any effort to help the child grow, develop, learn and be reasonably free from stress and tension must take this dominance of movement in the life of the child into account.

Practically all children—unless there is an incapacitating impairment—will engage in physical activity if given the opportunity to do so. They run, jump, climb and play games requiring these movement skills. Some adults consider this so-called "free play" meaningless. On the contrary, it is very meaningful to children as they explore various ways to move their bodies through space. In addition, to this unorganized form of activity, there are various types of organized physical activity programs for children. In general, these can be classified into the two broad categories of: (1) school programs, and (2) out-of-school programs.

**School Programs**

Most better-than-average elementary schools try to provide for well-balanced physical education programs for children. Just as young children need to learn the basic skills of reading, writing and mathematics, they should also learn the basic physical skills. These include: (1) locomotor skills of walking, running, leaping, jumping, hopping, galloping, skipping and sliding; (2) the auxiliary skills of starting, stopping, dodging, pivoting, landing and falling; and (3) the skills of propulsion and retrieval involving throwing, striking, kicking and catching.

For the young child, being able to move as effectively and efficiently as possible is directly related to the proficiency with which he or she will be able to perform the various fundamental physical skills. In turn, the success that children have in physical education activities requiring certain motor skills will be dependent upon their proficiency of performance of these skills. Thus, effective and efficient movement is prerequisite to the performance of basic motor skills needed for success in school physical education activities. These activities include active games, rhythmic activities and gymnastic activities. (Parents are advised to explore the extent to which a given school provides for such physical activities for children.)

### Out-of-School Programs

Out-of-school programs are provided by various organizations such as boys' and girls' clubs and neighborhood recreation centers. These programs vary in quality depending upon the extent of suitable facilities and qualified personnel available to supervise and conduct them. Parents should investigate these programs thoroughly to make sure they are being conducted in the best interests of children. This is mentioned because some highly competitive sports programs for children place more emphasis on adult pride than on the welfare of children. This should not be interpreted as an indictment against all out-of-school programs because many of them are doing a commendable job.

Some families do not rely on any kind of organized out-of-school program, preferring instead to plan their own activities. They make a valid effort to provide activities on their own. This is commendable because it can make for fine family relationships as well as provide for wholesome physical activity for the entire family. There is much truth to the old adage: "The family that plays together stays together."

Up to this point in this discussion, we have been thinking pretty much in terms of school age children. However, in recent years in keeping with the so-called "exercise craze," more and more emphasis has been placed on physical activity and exercise for "very tiny tots." Beginning some years ago the "water babies" program which is concerned with teaching infants to swim, met with much success. More recently the infant exercise concept has prompted widespread interest. One such program call *Gymboree* was started in 1976 by Joan Barnes, a former dance instructor from Burlingame, California. Growing at a very rapid rate, this program is divided into three sessions according to a child's age: (1) *BabyGym*—for infants three months to one year with parents helping their children with choreographed exercises such as bicycling legs or stretching arms; (2) *Gymboree*—for children from one year to 18 months with time devoted to "free exploration" and some structured time for songs, fingerplays and creative movements; and (3) *GymGrad*—for preschoolers two and one half to four years using "Gymbercises," a combination of stretches, body awareness, and aerobics and following a different theme each week. Although lacking in solid objective scientific evidence to support its value, in general, parents have given much empirical support to this approach. Many parents report that after engaging in these activities with their children, they feel much more relaxed themselves. Thus, it is possible that this type of program provides for therapy for parents as well as the physical well-being of their children.

## REST AND SLEEP

To be effective in life pursuits, periodic recuperation is an essential ingredient in daily living patterns. Rest and sleep provide us with the means of revitalizing ourselves to meet the challenges of our responsibilities.

In order to keep fatigue at a minimum and in its proper proportion in the cycle of everyday activities, nature has provided us with ways that help combat and reduce it. First, however, we should consider what fatigue is so that it may then be easier for us to cope with it.

There are two types of fatigue, *acute* and *chronic*. Acute fatigue is a natural outcome of sustained or severe exertion. It is due to such physical factors as the accumulation of by-products of muscular exertion in the blood and to excessive "oxygen debt"—the inability of the body to take in as much oxygen as is being consumed by muscular work. Psychological considerations may also be important in acute fatigue. That is, an individual who becomes bored with his work and who becomes preoccupied with the discomfort involved will become "fatigued" much sooner than if he is highly motivated to do the same work, is not bored, and does not think about the discomfort.

Activity that brings on distressing acute fatigue in one individual may amount to mild, even pleasant, exertion in another. The difference in fatigue level is due essentially to the physical fitness; that is, training, of the individual for the particular work under consideration. Thus, a good walker or dancer may soon become fatigued when running or swimming hard. The key, then, to controlling acute fatigue is sufficient training, in the activities to be engaged in, to prevent premature and undue fatigue. Knowing one's limits at any given time is also important as a guide to avoiding excessively fatiguing exertion and to determining what preparatory training is necessary.

Chronic fatigue has reference to fatigue which lasts over extended periods—in contrast with acute fatigue, which tends to be followed by a recovery phase and restoration to "normal" within a more or less brief period of time. Chronic fatigue may be due to any and a variety of medical conditions ranging from a disease to malnutrition (such conditions are the concern of the physician who, incidentally, should evaluate all cases of chronic fatigue to assure that a disease condition is not responsible). It may also be due to psychological factors such as extreme boredom and/or worry of having to do, over an extended period, what one does not wish to do.

Rest and sleep are essential to life as they afford the body the chance to regain its vitality and efficiency in a very positive way. Learning to utilize opportunities for rest and sleep may add years to our lives and zest to our years. Although rest and sleep are closely allied, they are not synonymous. For this reason it seems appropriate to consider them separately.

### Rest

In general, most people think of rest as just "taking it easy." A chief purpose of rest is to reduce tension so that the body may be better able to recover from fatigue. There is no overt activity involved, but neither is there loss of consciousness as in sleep. In rest, there is no loss of awareness of the external environment as in sleep. Since the need for rest is usually in direct proportion to the type of activity in which we engage, it follows naturally that the more strenuous the activity, the more frequent the rest periods should be. A busy day at school or on the job may not be as noticeably active as a game of tennis, nevertheless, it is the wise person who will let the body dictate when a rest period is required. Five or ten minutes of sitting in a chair with eyes closed may make the difference in the course of an active day, assuming of course that this is possible. The real effectiveness of rest periods depends largely on the individual and his or her ability to let down and rest.

## Sleep

Sleep is a phenomenon that has never been clearly defined or understood but has aptly been named the "great restorer." It is no wonder that authorities on the subject agree that sleep is essential to the vital functioning of the body and that natural sleep is the most satisfying form of recuperation from fatigue. It is during the hours of sleep that the body is given an opportunity to revitalize itself. All vital functions are slowed down so that the building of new cells and the repair of tissues can take place without undue interruption. This does not mean that the body builds and regenerates tissue only during sleep, but it does mean that it is the time that nature has set aside to accomplish the task more easily. The body's metabolic rate is lowered and energy is restored.

Despite the acknowledged need for sleep, a question of paramount importance concerns the amount of sleep necessary for the body to accomplish its recuperative task. There is no clear-cut answer to this query. Sleep is an individual matter, based on degree rather than kind. The usual recommendation for adults is eight hours of sleep out of every 24, but the basis for this could well be one of fallacy rather than fact. There are many persons who can function effectively on much less sleep, while others require more. No matter how many hours of sleep you get during the course of a 24 hour period, the best test of adequacy will depend largely on how you feel. If you are normally alert, feel healthy, and are in good humor, you are probably getting a sufficient amount of sleep. The rest that sleep normally brings to the body depends to a large extent upon a person's freedom from excessive emotional tension and ability to relax. Unrelaxed sleep has little restorative value, but learning to relax is a skill that is not acquired in one night.

Is loss of sleep dangerous? This is a question that is pondered quite frequently. Again, the answer is not simple. To the normally

healthy person with normal sleep habits, an occasional missing of
the accustomed hours of sleep is not serious. On the other hand,
repeated loss of sleep over a period of time can be dangerous. It is
the loss of sleep night after night, rather than at one time, that
apparently does the damage and results in the condition previously
described as chronic fatigue. The general effects of loss of sleep are
likely to result in poor general health, nervousness, irritability,
inability to concentrate, lowered perseverance of effort, and serious fatigue. Studies have shown that a person can go for much
longer periods of time without food than without sleep. In some
instances successive loss of sleep for long periods have proven
fatal. Under normal conditions, however, a night of lost sleep
followed by a period of prolonged sleep will restore the individual
to his normal self.

There are many conditions than tend to rob the body of restful
slumber. Most certainly, mental anguish and worry play a very
large part in holding sleep at bay. Some factors that influence the
quality of sleep are hunger, cold, boredom, and excessive fatigue.
In many instances these factors can be controlled. Incidentally,
Robert Coursey[7] a psychologist at the University of Maryland
and a researcher of sleep, has indicated that people who are
"insomniacs" may only think they are, and one of the things that
insomniacs worry about incessively is their sleepless condition.
His definition of a chronic insomniac is one who takes longer to
fall asleep, has more trouble staying asleep, wakes up earlier than
a normal sleeper and feels tired as a result. In any case, insomnia
and chronic fatigue might well be brought to the attention of a
physician so that the necessary steps can be taken to bring about
restoration of normal sleep patterns. Certainly, drugs to induce
sleep should be utilized only if prescribed by a physician.

Some recommendations about sleep might include: (1) relaxing
physically and mentally before retiring, (2) reducing tension levels
during the day, (3) managing your time, activities and thoughts to
prepare for a good night's sleep, and (4) the process should be the
same each night, and should begin at the same hour, leading to

---

[7]Coursey, Robert, "To Sleep or Not to Sleep—That is the Problem," *Precis*, College Park,
Maryland, September 12, 1977.

repose at the same hour. That is, if one's bedtime is normally eleven o'clock preparation should perhaps begin at least by ten and probably not later than ten-thirty.

## Sleeping Habits of Children

During the first year of a child's life it is a common practice to have two nap periods, one in the morning and one in the afternoon. The year-old child ordinarily, but gradually, gives up his morning nap and this tends to increase his afternoon nap time as well as his night sleep. With age the child will decrease his afternoon nap time and as a consequence he will sleep longer at night. Although there is some difference of opinion on when a child should give up both the morning and afternoon nap, it is generally considered that preschoolers should have at least one nap a day, preferably in the afternoon.

As in the case of adults, school age children differ in the number of hours of sleep required. The general recommendation is that on average out of every 24 hours they should get ten hours of sleep. A very important factor is that bedtime should be a happy time. Adults should not make such an issue of it that conflict results. Perhaps a good rule for a younger child is that he be "taken" to bed rather than "sent." The ceremony of reading or telling the child a pleasant story at bedtime is important and can help lessen the impact of sudden separation. It is important to remember that some of the sleep disorders of children can be traced directly to stressful conditions under which separation at bedtime occurs.

In closing this chapter we remind the reader that understanding the complex nature of sleep may be the province of scientists and other qualified experts, but an understanding of the value of sleep is the responsibility of everyone.

# CHAPTER 6

# CONTROLLING EMOTIONS

CONTROL YOURSELF!!! This is a common expression and it is very likely that more often than not it is used in reference to emotional restraint. At one time or another all of us, children and adults alike, demonstrate emotional behavior as well as ordinary behavior. Differences in the individual person and the environment will likely govern the degree to which each individual child expresses emotional behavior.

Adults should not think in terms of always suppressing the emotions of children. On the contrary, the goal should be to help children express their emotions as harmlessly as possible when they do occur so that emotional stability will be maintained. If this can be accomplished, the stress resulting from harmful emotional behavior can at least be reduced, if not eliminated entirely.

Emotional stress can be brought about by the stimulus of any of the emotional patterns. For example, the emotional pattern of anger can be stimulated by such factors as the thwarting of one's wishes, or a number of cumulative irritations. Response to such stimuli can be either *impulsive* or *inhibited.* An impulsive expression of anger is one that is directed against a person or an object, while the inhibited expressions are kept under some restraint but may be shown in such overt behavior as skin flushing.

Generally speaking, emotional patterns can be placed into the two broad categories of *pleasant* emotions and *unpleasant* emotions. Pleasant emotional patterns include such things as joy, affection, happiness and love in the broad sense, while included among the unpleasant emotional patterns are anger, sorrow, jealousy, fear and worry — an imaginary form of fear. The pleasantness or unpleasantness of an emotion seems to be determined by its strength or intensity, by the nature of the situation arousing it, and by the way the child perceives or interprets the situation.

108

The ancient Greeks identified emotions with certain organs of the body. For example, in general, sorrow was expressed from the heart (a broken heart), jealousy was associated with the liver, hate with the gall bladder and anger with the spleen. In regard to the latter, we sometimes hear the expression "wreaking the spleen" on someone. This historical reference is made because in modern times we take into account certain conduits between the emotions and the body. These are by way of the nervous system and the endocrine systems. That part of the nervous system principally concerned with the emotions is the *autonomic* nervous system which controls functions such as the heartbeat, blood pressure, and digestion. When there is a stimulus of any of the emotional patterns these two systems activate. By way of illustration, if the emotional pattern of fear is stimulated, the heartbeat accelerates, breathing is more rapid and the blood pressure is likely to rise. Energy fuel is discharged into the blood from storage in the liver which causes the blood sugar level to rise. These, along with other bodily functions serve to prepare a person to cope with the condition caused by the fear.

Dealing with childhood emotions should imply that sympathetic guidance should be provided in meeting anxieties, joys, and sorrow and that help should be given in developing aspirations and security. In order to attempt to reach this objective, we might consider emotions from a standpoint of the growing child maturing emotionally.

For purposes of this discussion, *maturity* will be considered as a state of *readiness* on the part of the child. The term is most frequently used in connection with age relationships. For example, it may be said that "Johnny is mature for six years of age." Simply stated, *emotional maturity* is the process of acting one's age.

In general, emotional maturity will be achieved through a gradual accumulation of mild and pleasant emotions. Emotional *im*maturity indicates that unpleasant emotions have accumulated too rapidly for the child to absorb. One of the important factors in this regard is the process of *adjustment,* which can be described as the process of finding and adopting modes of behavior suitable to the environment, or to changes in the environment.

The child's world involves a sequence of experiences that are characterized by the necessity for him to adjust. Consequently, it may be said that "normal" behavior is the result of successful adjustment, and abnormal behavior results from unsuccessful adjustment. The degree of adjustment that the child achieves depends upon how adequately he is able to satisfy his basic needs and to fulfill his desires within the framework of his environment and the pattern of ways dictated by society.

When stress is induced as a result of the child's not being able to meet his needs (basic demands) and satisfy his desires (wants or wishes), *conflict* or *frustration* result. Conflict occurs when (1) choices must be made between nearly equally attractive alternatives, or (2) when basic emotional forces oppose one another. Frustration occurs when a need is not met. In an emotionally healthy person, the degree of frustration is ordinarily in proportion to the intensity of the need or desire. That is, he will objectively observe and evaluate the situation to ascertain whether a solution is possible and, if so, what solution would best enable him to achieve the fulfillment of his needs or his desires. (Frustration is a major cause of *aggression* which will be discussed in detail later in the chapter.)

Every person has a *zone of tolerance* or limits for emotional stress within which he normally operates. If the stress becomes considerably greater than the tolerance level or if the individual has not learned to cope with his problems and to try to solve them intelligently, some degree of maladjustment can possibly result.

In order to counteract some of the above problems and to be able to pursue a sensible course in helping children become more emotionally mature, there are certain factors concerned with emotional development of children that need to be taken into account. Some of the factors are the subject of the following discussion.

## FACTORS CONCERNING EMOTIONAL DEVELOPMENT

Some of the factors concerned with emotional development of children that need to be considered are: (1) characteristics of childhood emotionality, (2) emotional arousals and reactions, and (3) factors that influence emotionality.

## Characteristics of Childhood Emotionality

**Ordinarily, the emotions of children are not long lasting.** A child's emotions may last for a few minutes and then terminate rather abruptly. The child gets it "out of his system," so to speak, by expressing it outwardly. In contrast, some adult emotions may be long and drawn out. As children get older, expressing the emotions by overt action is encumbered by certain social restraints. This is to say that what might be socially acceptable at one age level is not necessarily so at another. This may be a reason for some children developing *moods,* which in a sense are states of emotion drawn out over a period of time and expressed slowly. Typical moods of childhood may be "sulking" due to restraint or anger, being "jumpy" from repressed fear, and becoming "humorous" from controlled joy or happiness.

**The emotions of children are likely to be intense.** This might be confusing to some adults who do not understand child behavior; that is, they may not be able to see why a child would react rather violently to a situation that to them might appear insignificant.

**The emotions of children are subject to rapid change.** A child is capable of shifting rapidly from laughing to crying or from anger to joy. Although the reason for this is not definitely known, it might be that there is not as much depth of feeling among children as there is among adults. In addition, it could be due to lack of experience that children have had, as well as their state of intellectual development. We do know that young children have a short attention span that could cause them to change rapidly from one kind of emotion to another.

**The emotions of children can appear with a high degree of frequency.** As children get older they manage to develop the ability to adjust to situations that previously would have caused an emotional reaction. This is probably due to the child's acquiring more experience with various kinds of emotional situations. Perhaps a child learns through experience what is socially acceptable and what is socially unacceptable. This is particularly true if the child is reprimanded in some way following a violent emotional reaction. For this reason, the child may try to confront situations in ways that do not involve an emotional response.

**Children differ in their emotional responses.** One child confronted with a situation that instills fear may run away from the immediate environment. Another may hide behind his mother. Still another might just stand there and cry. Different reactions of children to emotional situations are probably due to a host of factors. Included among these may be past experiences with a certain kind of emotional situation, willingness of parents and other adults to help children become independent, and family relationships in general.

**Strength of children's emotions are subject to change.** At some age levels certain kinds of emotions may be weak and later become stronger. Conversely, with some children emotions that were strong may tend to decline. For example, small children may be timid among strangers, but later when they see that there is nothing to fear, the timidity is likely to wane.

### Emotional Arousals and Reactions

If we are to understand the emotions of children, we need to take into account those factors of emotional arousal and how children might be expected to react to them. Many different kinds of emotional patterns have been identified. For purposes here we have arbitrarily selected for discussion the emotional states of fear, worry, anger, jealousy and joy.

**Fear.** It is possible that it is not necessarily the arousal itself but rather the way something is presented that determines whether there will be a fear reaction. For example, if a child is trying to perform a stunt and the discussion is in terms of "if you do it that way you will break your neck," it is possible a fear response will occur. This is one of the many reasons for using a positive approach in dealing with children.

A child may react to fear by withdrawing. With very young children this may be in the form of crying or breath holding. With a child under three years of age and in some older children as well, the "ostrich" approach may be used; that is, he may hide his face in order to get away from it. As children get older, these forms of reactions may decrease or cease altogether because of social pressures. For instance, it may be considered "sissy" to cry, especially among boys. (The validity of this kind of thinking is of course open to question.)

**Worry.** This might be considered an imaginary form of fear, and it can be a fear not aroused directly from the child's environment. Worry can be aroused by imagining a situation that could possibly arise; that is, a child could worry about not being able to perform well in a certain activity. Since worries are likely to be caused by imaginary rather than real conditions, they are not likely to be found in abundance among very young children. Perhaps the reason for this is that they have not reached a stage of intellectual development at which they might imagine certain things that could cause worry. While children will respond to worry in different ways, certain manifestations such as nail biting may be symptomatic of this condition.

**Anger.** This emotional response tends to occur more frequently than that of fear. This is probably because there are more conditions that incite anger. In addition, some children quickly learn that anger may get attention that otherwise would not be forthcoming. It is likely that as children get older they may show more anger responses than fear responses because they soon see that there is not too much to fear.

Anger is caused by many factors, one of which is interference with movements the child wants to execute. This interference can come from others or by the child's own limitations in ability and physical development.

Because of individual differences in children, there is a wide variation in anger responses. As mentioned previously, these responses are either *impulsive* or *inhibited.* In impulsive responses, the child manifests an overt action either toward another person or an object that caused the anger. For instance, a child who collides with a door might take out the anger by kicking or hitting the door. (This form of child behavior is also sometimes manifested by some "adults.") Inhibited responses are likely to be kept under control, and as children mature emotionally, they acquire more ability to control their anger.

**Jealousy.** This response usually occurs when a child feels a threat of loss of affection. Many psychologists believe that jealousy is closely related to anger. Because of this, the child may build up resentment against another person. Jealousy can be devastating in childhood, and every effort should be made to avoid it.

Jealousy is concerned with social interaction that involves persons the child likes. These individual can be parents, siblings, teachers, and peers. There are various ways in which the child may respond. These include: (1) being aggressive toward the one of whom one is jealous or possibly toward others as well, (2) withdrawing from the person whose affections he thinks have been lost, and (3) possible development of an "I don't care" attitude.

In some cases children will not respond in any of the above ways. They might try to excel over the person of whom they are jealous or they might tend to do things to impress the person whose affections they thought had been lost.

**Joy.** This pleasant emotion is one for which we strive because it is so important in maintaining emotional stability. Causes of joy differ from one age level to another and from one child to another at the same age level. This is to say that what might be a joyful situation for one person might not necessarily be so for another.

Joy is expressed in various ways, but the most common are laughing and smiling, the latter being a restrained form of laughter. Some people respond to joy with a state of relaxation. This is difficult to detect because it has little or no overt manifestation. Nevertheless, it may be noticed when one compares it with body tension caused by unpleasant emotions.

### Factors That Influence Emotionality

If we can consider that a child is emotionally fit when his emotions are properly controlled and he is becoming emotionally mature, then emotional fitness is dependent to a certain extent upon certain factors that influence emotionality in childhood. The following is a descriptive list of some of these factors.

**Fatigue.** As mentioned in the preceding chapter, there are two types of fatigue, *acute* and *chronic*. Acute fatigue is a natural outcome of sustained severe exertion. It is due to physical factors such as the accumulation of the by products of muscular exertion in the blood and to excessive *oxygen debt*—the ability of the body to take in as much oxygen as is being consumed by the muscular work. Psychological considerations may also be important in acute fatigue. That is, an individual, who becomes bored with his work and who becomes preoccupied with the discomfort involved, will become "fatigued" much sooner than if he is highly motivated to do the same work, is not bored, and does not think about the discomfort.

Chronic fatigue has reference to fatigue that lasts over extended periods, in contrast to acute fatigue, which tends to be followed by a recovery phase and restoration to "normal" within a more or less brief period of time. Chronic fatigue may be due to any or a variety of medical conditions ranging from a disease such as tuberculosis to malnutrition. (Such conditions are the concern of the physician who, incidentally, should evaluate all cases of chronic fatigue in order to assure that a disease condition is not responsible.) It may also be due to psychological factors such as extreme boredom and/or worry of having to do what one does not wish to do over an extended period.

Fatigue predisposes children to irritability; consequently, actions are taken to ward if off such as having rest periods or, in the case of the nursery school, fruit juice periods. In this particular regard, some studies show that the hungrier a child is, the more prone he may be to outbursts of anger.

**Inferior health status.** The same thing holds true here as in the case of fatigue. Temporary poor health, such as colds and the like, tends to make children irritable. There are studies that show that there are fewer emotional outbursts among healthy than unhealthy children.

**Intelligence.** Studies tend to show that, on the average, children of low intellectual levels have less emotional control than children with higher levels of intelligence. This may be because there may be less frustration if a child is intelligent enough to figure things out. The reverse could also be true because children with high level intelligence are better able to perceive things that would be likely to arouse emotions.

**Social environment.** In a social environment where such things as quarreling and unrest exist, a child is predisposed to unpleasant emotional conditions. Likewise, school schedules that are too crowded can cause undue emotional excitation among children.

**Family relationships.** There are a variety of conditions concerned with family relationships that can influence childhood emotionality. Among others, these include: (1) parental neglect, (2) overanxious parents, and (3) over-protective parents.

**Aspiration levels.** It can make for an emotionally unstable situation if parent expectations are beyond a child's ability. In addition, children who have not been made aware of their own limitations may set goals too high and as a result have too many failures.

All of these factors can have a negative influence on childhood emotionality, and thus, possibly induce emotional stress. Therefore, efforts should be made as far as possible to eliminate the negative aspects of these factors. Those that cannot be completely eliminated should at least be kept under control.

## AGGRESSION

Aggression literally means "to attack." It is ordinarily provoked by anger and results in hostile action. Thus, anger is the emotional pattern and it is outwardly demonstrated by aggression.

In recent years there has been a systematic effort to study childhood aggression — its causes, how it is learned, and how it can be controlled. One of the most profound and detailed of these studies was reported at the 91st meeting of the American Psychological Association in 1983.

This 20-year study indicated that lifetime habits of aggressive behavior are already pretty firmly established in children by eight years of age. It appears that most aggressive children learn their behavior from their parents and also from watching violent television programs early in life.

This study which began in 1960 with almost 900 third grade children showed that those rated as the most aggressive at that time were likely to be rated the same way 10 and 20 years later. Moreover, they also were three times more likely than their less aggressive classmates to be convicted of serious crimes by age 30. The striking thing about this is that if nothing is done to change the behavior of young children, these bad habits will carry over into adulthood.

A great deal of fault lies with parents who demonstrate aggressive behavior toward their children. For example, continued harsh punishment for aggressive behavior tends to increase aggression, rather than diminish it. It is interesting to note that girls were found to be far less aggressive than boys which is perhaps due to the fact that parents, particularly fathers, have a much higher level of expectancy as far as boys are concerned.

Various other studies of childhood aggression have been conducted over the years and the following is a list of generalizations derived from these findings.

1. **Children rewarded for aggression learn that aggression pays off.** This generalization is concerned with the extent to which an adult uses praise for achievement. The adult must be able to quickly determine whether success was due more to aggressive behavior than skill or ability. The important thing here is the extent of aggressive behavior. Certainly an adult should not thwart enthusiasm. It is sometimes difficult to determine whether an act was due to genuine enthusiasm or to undesirable aggressive behavior.

2. **Children involved in constructive activities may be less likely to behave aggressively.** In the school setting this implies that lessons should be well-planned so that time is spent on constructive learning activities. When this is accomplished it will be more likely that desirable and worthwhile learning will take place.

3. **Children who have alternative responses readily available are less likely to resort to aggression to get what they want.** This is concerned essentially with adult-child relationships. While the school environment generally involves group situations, there are many "one-on-one" opportunities between teacher and child. This situation pertains as well to the home environment if a parent is willing to spend time on these one-on-one relationships. This gives an adult a chance to tell the child the kind of behavior that is expected under certain conditions. For example, a child who *asks* for an object such as a ball is more likely to receive cooperation. A child who *grabs* the ball is more likely to provoke aggression on the part of the other child. Teaching reinforcement can increase a child's use of nonaggressive solutions to interpersonal problems.

The adult should be ready to intervene in a potentially aggressive situation before aggression occurs, encouraging children to use nonaggressive methods to solve conflicts. Verbal alternatives can be provided for those children who do not think of them. For example, "I am playing with this now," or "You can ask him to trade with you."

4. **Children imitate behavior of people they like, and they often adopt an adult's behavior.** Teachers are more likely to be a model adopted by children than would be the case with most other adults, sometimes including parents. One of the reasons is that many children like to try to please their teachers and tend to make serious efforts to do so. Of course it is helpful if a teacher is nonaggressive in his or her own behavior.

5. **Cooperation may be incompatible with aggression.** This could be interpreted to mean that an adult should consistently attend to and reinforce all cooperative behavior. Children consistently reinforced for cooperative behavior are likely to increase cooperative interactions while simultaneously decreasing aggressive behavior.

Before closing this section of the chapter, it is important that we point out the difference between aggressive behavior and *assertive* behavior. The latter form of behavior has received a great deal of attention in recent years, and rightly so. Self-assertiveness should be considered as a basic role in one's life. All of us, adults and children, have a need for self-reliance and confidence in our abilities. This need can be met by asserting ourselves in a manner that we pursue our personal goals without too much dependence on others. Certainly one can be assertive without being aggressive.

## GUIDELINES FOR
## EMOTIONAL DEVELOPMENT OF CHILDREN

It is important to set forth some guidelines for emotional development if adults are to meet with any degree of success in their efforts to provide for emotional development of children. The reason for this is to assure, at least to some extent, that attempts to attain optimum emotional development will be based more or less on a scientific approach. The guidelines can take the form of valid *concepts of emotional development.* This approach enables us to give serious consideration to what is known about how children grow and develop emotionally. The following list of concepts of emotional development is submitted with this general idea in mind.

1. **An emotional response may be brought about by a goal's being furthered or thwarted.** Adults should make a very serious effort to assure successful experiences for every child. In the school setting this can be accomplished in part by attempting to provide for individual differences within given school experiences. The school or home setting should be such that each child derives of feeling of personal worth through making some sort of positive contribution.

2. **Self-realization experiences should be constructive.** The opportunity for creative experiences that afford the child a chance for self-realization should be inherent in all of his environments. In the school setting teachers might well consider planning with children to see that all school activities are meeting their needs, and as a result, involve constructive experiences.

3. **Emotional responses increase as the development of the child brings greater awareness and the ability to remember the past and to anticipate the future.** Children can be reminded of their past pleasant emotional responses with words of praise. This could encourage children to repeat such responses in future similar situations.

4. **As the child develops, the emotional reactions tend to become less violent and more discriminating.** A well planned program of school experiences and wholesome home activities should be such that they provide for release of aggression in a socially acceptable manner.

5. **Emotional reactions tend to increase beyond normal expectancy toward the constructive or destructive reactions on the balance of furthering or hindering experiences of the child.** For some children the confidence they need to be able to face the problems of life may come through physical expression. Therefore, experiences such as active play in the home surroundings and good physical education programs in the schools have tremendous potential to help contribute toward a solid base of total development.

6. **Depending on certain factors, a child's own feelings may be accepted or rejected by the individual.** Children's environmental experiences should make them feel good and have confidence in themselves. Satisfactory self-concept is closely related to body control; physical activity oriented experiences might be consid-

ered as one of the ways of contributing to it. Therefore, it is important to consider those kinds of experiences for young children that will provide them with the opportunity for a certain degree of freedom of movement.

## OPPORTUNITIES FOR EMOTIONAL DEVELOPMENT IN THE VARIOUS ENVIRONMENTS

The home, school, camp and other environments have the potential to provide for emotional stability. The extent to which this actually occurs is dependent primarily on the kind of emotional climate provided by the adult in charge of the environment. For this reason it appears pertinent to examine some of the potential opportunities that exist for emotional development in the child's environments. The following descriptive list is submitted for this purpose. It should be borne in mind that these opportunities will not happen automatically, but that adults need to work constantly to try to make such conditions a reality.

1. **Release of aggression in a socially acceptable manner.** This appears to be an outstanding way in which school activities such as physical education can help to make children more secure and emotionally stable. For example, kicking a ball in a game of kickball, batting a softball, or engaging in a combative stunt can afford a socially acceptable way of releasing aggression. The same can be said for a home environment where parents provide their children with wholesome recreation and active play opportunities.

2. **Inhibition of direct response of unpleasant emotions.** This statement does not necessarily mean that feelings concerned with such unpleasant emotions as fear and anger should be completely restrained. On the contrary the interpretation should be that such feelings can take place less frequently in a wholesome environment. This means that opportunities should be provided to relieve tension rather than to aggravate it.

3. **Promotion of pleasant emotions.** Perhaps there is too much concern with suppressing unpleasant emotions and not enough attention given to promotion of pleasant ones. This means that the environment should provide a range of activities through

which all children can succeed. Thus, all children, regardless of ability, should be afforded the opportunity for success, at least some of the time.

**4. Recognition of one's abilities and limitations.** It has already been mentioned that a wide range of activities should provide an opportunity for success for all. This should make it easier in the school setting to provide for individual differences of children so that all of them can progress within the limits of their own skill and ability.

**5. Understanding about the ability and achievements of others.** Emphasis can be placed upon achievements of the group, along with the function of each individual in the group. Team play and group effort is important in most situations.

**6. Being able to make a mistake without being unduly criticized.** In the school setting this requires that the teacher serve as a catalyst who helps children understand the idea of trial and error. Emphasis can be placed on *trying* and that one can learn not only from his own mistakes but also from the mistakes of others. The same approach can apply equally well in the home situation.

This discussion has included just a few examples of the numerous opportunities to help provide for emotional development in the child's particular environment. The resourceful and creative adult should be able to expand this list manyfold.

## EVALUATING INFLUENCES OF THE ENVIRONMENT ON EMOTIONAL DEVELOPMENT

What we are essentially concerned with here is how an adult can make some sort of valid evaluation of the extent to which the particular environment contributes to emotional development. This means that the adult should make some attempt to assess experiences with reference to whether or not these experiences are providing for emotional maturity.

One approach would be to refer to the "opportunities for emotional development in the various environments" just discussed. These opportunities have been converted into a rating scale and

may be used by an adult to assess the extent to which experiences
in the environment provide for emotional development.

  1. The experiences provide for release of aggression in a socially
     acceptable manner.
       4 most of the time
       3 some of the time
       2 occasionally
       1 infrequently
  2. The experiences provide for inhibition of direct response of
     unpleasant emotions.
       4 most of the time
       3 some of the time
       2 occasionally
       1 infrequently
  3. The experiences provide for promotion of pleasant emotions.
       4 most of the time
       3 some of the time
       2 occasionally
       1 infrequently
  4. The experiences provide for recognition of one's abilities
     and limitations.
       4 most of the time
       3 some of the time
       2 occasionally
       1 infrequently
  5. The experiences provide for an understanding about the
     ability and achievement of others.
       4 most of the time
       3 some of the time
       2 occasionally
       1 infrequently
  6. The experiences provide for being able to make a mistake
     without being unduly criticized.
       4 most of the time
       3 some of the time
       2 occasionally
       1 infrequently

If one makes these ratings objectively and conscientiously, a reasonably good procedure for evaluation is provided. Ratings can be made periodically to see if positive changes appear to be taking place. Also, they can be made for a single experience, a group of experiences, or for the total of all experiences. This procedure can help to identify the extent to which experiences and/or conditions under which the experiences take place are contributing to emotional development.

## THE MYTHICAL EMOTIONALLY HEALTHY PERSON

This heading is not meant to imply that emotional health is a myth. What we are thinking about is the identification of characteristics of *ideal* emotionally healthy persons. Looking at some of these characteristics, one must understand that they are neither absolute nor static. Individuals are not always happy, and they sometimes find themselves in situations where they are not overly confident. In fact, sometimes all of us may feel downright inadequate to solve commonplace problems that occur in our daily lives.

1. Emotionally healthy persons have achieved basic harmony within themselves and a workable relationship with others. They are able to function effectively, and usually happily, even though they are well aware of the limitations and rigors involved in human existence.

2. Emotionally healthy persons manage to adapt to the demands of environmental conditions with emotional responses that are appropriate in degree and kind to the stimuli and situations and that fall, generally, within the range of what is considered "normal" within various environments.

3. Emotionally healthy persons face problems directly and seek realistic and plausible solutions to them. They try to free themselves from excessive and unreal anxieties, worries, and fears, even though they are aware that there is much to be concerned with and much to be anxious about in our complex modern society.

4. Emotionally healthy persons have developed a guiding philosophy of life and have a set of values that are acceptable to

themselves and that are generally in harmony with those values of society that are reasonable and conducive to human happiness.

5. Emotionally healthy persons accept themselves and are willing to deal with the world as it exists in reality. They accept what cannot be changed at a particular time and place and they build and derive satisfaction within the framework of their own potentialities and those of their environment.

6. Emotionally healthy persons tend to be happy, and they tend to have an enthusiasm for living. They do not focus their attention exclusively upon what they consider to be their inadequacies, weaknesses, and "bad" qualities. They view those around them this way too.

7. Emotionally healthy persons have a variety of satisfying interests and they maintain a balance between their work, routine responsibilities, and recreation. They find constructive and satisfying outlets for creative expression in the interests that they undertake.

We repeat that this list of characteristics of emotionally healthy persons presents a near-ideal situation and obviously none of us operate at these high levels at all times. However, they might well be considered as suitable guidelines for which we might strive to help, not only children, but ourselves as well to deal with and possibly prevent unpleasant emotional stress.

## CHAPTER 7

# CONTROLLING FEARS

In the preceding chapter, although we identified fear as an emotional pattern, we did not define or describe it. The term *fear* from the Old English *fir* may have been derived originally from the German word *fahr*, meaning danger or peril. In modern times fear is often thought of in terms of anxiety caused by present or impending danger or peril. For example, one authoritative source[1] suggests that fear is generally defined as a normal and specific reaction to a genuine threat, which is present at the moment. Anxiety is usually defined as a more generalized reaction to a vague sense of threat in absence of a specific or realistic dangerous object. However, the terms are often used loosely and almost interchangeably. When fearful or anxious, individuals experience unpleasant changes in overt behavior, subjective feelings (including thoughts), and physiological activity.

Similarly, another source[2] contends that fears differ from anxiety in that the former are negative emotional responses to *specific* situations or objects, such as speaking before a group or receiving an injection, whereas the latter is an emotional state that tends to be prolonged and may be difficult to link to any specific environmental factor. But fears and anxiety are similar in the feelings they arouse: rapid heartbeat, sweating, quivering, heavy breathing, feeling week or numb in the limbs, dizziness or faintness, muscular tension, the need to eliminate, and a sense of dread—the "fight or flight" mechanism. Not all people experience

---

[1]Whitehead, D'Ann, Shirley, Mariela and Walker C. Eugene, Use of Systematic Desensitization in the Treatment of Children's Fears, In *Stress in Childhood*, Ed. James H. Humphrey, New York, AMS Press, Inc., 1984, p. 213.

[2]Rathus, Spencer A., and Nevid, Jeffrey S., *Behavior Therapy*, New York, New American Library, 1977, p. 36.

all these signs of fear, but most experience some of them.

Fears are common among children, particularly in early childhood. Examples of such fears are fear of dogs, insects, the dark and going to school. Childhood fears sometimes appear to be unexplainable and children have marked individual differences in susceptibility to fear. However, there is evidence that children display a definite tendency to learn adult's fears through identification with them or simply by observing them engage in fearful behavior. For example, if during a storm a child observes a parent being fearful, the child is likely to develop a similar fear and fear response pattern. On the other hand, many childhood fears are a function of direct contact or experience with frightening events (e.g., if the child were attacked by a dog). Parental warnings, without the parent necessarily being fearful of such, about certain objects or events (e.g., "watch out for strangers," "stay away from fires") may also lead to developmental fears in children.

Children's fears often tend not to be taken seriously by adults, because some adults generally hold the belief that children's fears "will pass" or that they will "grow out of them." However, it has been found that this may not always be the case, and that without treatment many fears may be maintained through adulthood.[3]

## CLASSIFICATION OF FEARS

There are various ways of classifying fears. Two prominent psychologists, Spencer Rathus and Jeffrey Nevid,[4] use the two broad classifications of *objective* fears and *irrational* fears.

### Objective Fears

Many fears are useful and necessary and it is logical that we be afraid of such things as:

---

[3]Whitehead, D'Ann, Shirley, Mariela and Walker, C. Eugene Use of Systematic Desensitization in the Treatment of Children's Fears, In *Stress in Childhood* Ed. James H. Humphrey, New York. AMS Press, Inc., p. 214, 216.

[4]Rathus, Spencer A., and Nevid, Jeffrey S., *Behavior Therapy*, New York, New American Library, 1977, p. 36–37.

touching a hot stove
falling from a high place
running into the street without looking for oncoming vehicles
receiving surgical procedures without benefit of anesthesia

These fears are said to be *rational* and *adaptive*.

### Irrational Fears

Some fears are said to be *irrational* and *maladaptive*. It is an irrational fear when the objective danger is disproportionate to the amount of distress experienced. These kinds of fears are called *phobias* or phobic disorders, among some of which are the following:

fear of high places, though one may be in no objective danger of falling
fear of closed-in, tight places when one is not necessarily in objective
    danger of being smothered or trapped
fear of receiving injections — not because of the potential minor pain, but
    because of the "thought" of the procedure
fear of working with sharp instruments
fear of the dark
fear of being alone

Irrational fears or phobias do not necessarily have to interfere with our lives. It matters little if you are afraid of heights if your life style permits you to avoid high places. Likewise, it matters little if you have a fear of snakes so long as your only encounter with them is likely to be a voluntary one at the zoo. However, some irrational fears can be debilitating experiences and interfere greatly with your attempt to lead your daily life. For instance, if you have no tolerance for the sight of blood or being in an environment of medical procedures, you may find your health or life endangered if you refrain from seeking treatment of an injury or disease. In such a case it would clearly be of benefit to do something about such fears.

## CONTROLLING FEARS THROUGH
## SYSTEMATIC SELF DESENSITIZATION

Systematic desensitization can be described as the process of systematically lessening a specific learned fear in an individual. It is purported to provide one means of controlling anxiety. If one can accomplish this, it becomes an extremely important factor in reducing stress. The reason for this is that the individual becomes more able to control his fears and anxieties, rather than having them control him.

From the point of view of a clinical psychotherapeutic procedure, systematic desensitization consists of presenting, to the imagination of the deeply relaxed person, the feeblest item in a list of anxiety-evoking stimuli repeatedly, until no more anxiety is evoked. The next item of the list is presented, and so on, until eventually, even the strongest of the anxiety-evoking stimuli fails to evoke any stir of anxiety in a person. It is the purpose of the remainder of this chapter to provide information on this technique. At the same time, we will give consideration to self-administration for the adult as well as how adults can use the technique to help control fears in children.

Originally, the focus of systematic desensitization was primarily upon counselor-client, therapist-patient, or teacher-student relationships, and it was perhaps one of the most widely used behavior therapy techniques. In recent years, systematic desensitization has gained tremendous favor as a self-administered technique. Although the value of it as a means of lessening stress-provoking situations has not been completely established by behavioral scientists, some of the research findings are indeed encouraging. For example, studies have shown that systematic self desensitization can be very effective in overcoming severe public speaking anxiety, test anxiety, and a host of other stress-invoking stimuli.

It has been suggested by one authoritative source[5] that systematic self desensitization efforts are not likely to be harmful, even if they fail. However, self desensitization should be approached as an experimental procedure and it should be discontinued if the course of anxiety-reduction is not relatively smooth, and it should be discontinued immediately if any increase of anxiety is experienced.

Various behavioral therapists and clinical psychologists have set forth procedures for adults for the practice of systematic self-

---

[5]Watson, David L., and Tharp, Roland G., *Self-Directed Behavior: Self Modification for Personal Adjustment*, Belmont, California, Wadsworth Publishing Company, Inc., 1972, p. 179.

desensitization. One impressive model which seems to have universal applicability is one suggested by one of our collaborators, C. Eugene Walker,[6] Chief, Pediatric Psychology, The University of Oklahoma Medical School.

The subject of systematic desensitization is introduced with the notion that many fears and anxieties that people experience are due to what are termed *conditioned reactions.* These conditioned reactions are identified as stimuli that occur together in our experience and become associated with each other so that we respond to them in the same way, or in a highly similar way, when they occur again. This is to say that if we are made anxious in the presence of certain stimuli these same stimuli will make us anxious later when they occur, even if the situation in reality no longer poses an actual threat. An example is a person who may have had a number of experiences as a child in which a person in authority, such as a school principal, policeman, or guard frightened him and perhaps punished him in some way. Such a person's reactions as an adult to one in authority may produce considerably more anxiety in him than the situation really warrants. This is because of his previous conditioning of strong anxiety to an authority figure.

Many of our emotions seem to be based on such conditioned reactions. And, these reactions are somewhat similar to reflexes, but they are learned rather than inherited (the reader is asked to refer back to the discussion of learned and unlearned tensions in Chapter 1). Their automatic or "reflexive" character, however, explains why it is difficult to discuss things rationally with someone who is emotionally involved in a situation. He is responding more with his conditioned reactions to the present stimuli than relating to the actual realities of a situation.

The recommendation for overcoming fears and anxieties in the form of conditioned reactions is the use of systematic self desensitization and a highly persuasive case can be made for its effectiveness—provided it is done properly.

---

[6]Walker, C. Eugene, *Learn to Relax, 13 Ways to Reduce Tension,* Englewood Cliffs, New Jersey, Prentice-Hall, Inc., 1975, p. 7.

## DESENSITIZING ADULTS TO FEAR

For most adults the procedure of systematic self desensitization is a relatively uncomplicated one. After a particular problem has been identified, the process consists of three sequential steps: (1) developing a hierarchy of anxiety-evoking stimuli, (2) complete relaxation, and (3) desensitization sessions. Using the previously mentioned authority figure as an example, let us make application of this to a "worker" who has difficulty with this problem where relationship with the "boss" is concerned.

The first step is to take several index cards, writing a different situation or experience on each card that makes for anxiety concerning the problem. The cards are then stacked in order with the one causing the least anxiety on the top and the one causing the greatest anxiety at the bottom. This is the hierarchy of anxiety-evoking stimuli and might resemble the following:

1. Entering parking lot and seeing the boss's car.
2. Greeting fellow workers and discussing the boss.
3. Greeting fellow worker who mentions his coming meeting with the boss.
4. Conferring with fellow worker after his meeting with the boss.
5. Walking by the boss's office when the door is closed.
6. Walking by the boss's office when the door is open (no verbalization or eye contact).
7. Walking by the boss's office when door is open using eye contact and nodding.
8. Arranging meeting with the boss's secretary.
9. Talking with the boss's secretary about the boss.
10. Pre-arranged meeting with the boss with secretary present.
11. Pre-arranged meeting with the boss with only self present.
12. Other meetings with the boss with only self present.

Another fear and possible stress inducing situation that occurs many times is that of making a report in front of a group. A hierarchy for this purpose follows:

1. Reading an article about giving reports.
2. Reading report alone.

3. Reading report in front of a mirror.
4. Reading report into tape recorder and playing back.
5. Reading report to fellow worker.
6. Reading report to a fellow worker with one other present.
7. Reading report with three others present.
8. Reading report to two or three others where there is a large gathering, such as the lunch room.
9. Entering a room where a report is being given.
10. Member of audience while other reports are given.
11. Giving report to entire group.

Of course the reader must understand that the above hierarchies of anxiety-evoking stimuli are general in nature and each individual would make out his or her own list in more specific detail and pertaining more to specific fears and anxieties.

The second step is to try to develop a condition of complete relaxation (the reader is referred to the following chapter for various relaxation procedures). It is recommended that the person go through each of the muscle groups in sequential order to learn to relax them one by one.

After the person is completely relaxed, the next step is the beginning of systematic self desensitization. This is done as follows: Look at the top card on the pile—the one that is the least anxiety provoking. Close the eyes, and using the imagination, visualize as vividly as possible the situation described on it. That is, one imagines the situation occurring and that he or she is actually there. At this point, if some anxiety is experienced, the imaginary scene should cease immediately and the person should go back to relaxing. After complete relaxation is again obtained, the person is ready to proceed. This procedure is continued until the scene can be imagined without anxiety. This may take only one or two times, or it could take 15 to 20 times, but it should be repeated until no anxiety is felt. The entire procedure is continued until one has gone through all the cards.

It is recommended that one work on the scenes in this manner for approximately one half hour at a time. It can be done daily, every other day, or a couple of times a week, depending upon the amount of time one is willing or able to spend, and how quickly one wants to conquer the anxiety. It appears to be a good practice to overlap one or two items from one session to another; that is, beginning a session by repeating an item or two from the previous session that were imagined without anxiety.

One variation of the above procedure is to tape record a description of each scene in advance. One then relaxes and listens to the tape. If anxiety appears, the recorder is turned off and the person goes back to relaxing. When relaxation is again accomplished the individual proceeds as before. A value of using the tape recorder is that there is likely to be better pronunciation, enunciation, and intonation of words. In addition, it may be easier for the individual to concentrate, since he has provided his own auditory input on tape and does not have the additional task of verbalizing and trying to concentrate on the scene at the same time. If desired, the sequence of relaxation procedures can be taped as well.

After one has been desensitized, he can review in his own mind the preferred action to take in the situation that caused anxiety. Plans can then be made to do the right thing the next time the situation occurs.

Obviously, the success one experiences with this procedure will depend largely upon the extent to which one is willing to make the painstaking effort involved in the approach. Many persons who have tried it have been so delighted by its effects that they have deliberately sought out situations that previously had caused them great anxiety, frustration and failure. This is certainly a true test of faith in the approach.

## DESENSITIZING CHILDREN TO FEAR

Systematic desensitization has been used with success in terms of lessening fears and anxieties among children. An example of such an experiment is one in which a six and one-half-year-old boy was unsuccessful in classroom verbalization.[7] Medical and psychiatric reports did not show any known reason for his un-

[7]Kravetz, R., and Forness, S., "The Special Classroom as a Desensitization Setting," *Exceptional Children*, 37(5) 389–391.

willingness to talk in the classroom. Although the child's test results revealed that he had ability above average, his school progress failed to reach his level of potential. A six-week desensitization program of two sessions per week was developed to try to reduce or eliminate his fear of verbalization in class. The following hierarchy of anxiety-evoking stimuli was used in the experiment.

1. Reading alone to investigator.
2. Reading alone to roommate.
3. Reading to two classroom aides.
4. Reading to teacher and classroom aides.
5. Reading to teacher, classroom aides, and small group of class peers.
6. Reading to entire class.
7. Asking questions or making comments at weekly meetings when all children, teachers, and staff were present.

This program of desensitization met with success in alleviating the child's fear of verbalization in the classroom. Other programs of this same general nature have been used to advantage in reducing test-taking anxiety, conquering the phobia of school attendance, fear of medical settings, fear of the dark, water, and insects — in fact most fears of children can be alleviated by systematic desensitization if the procedure is carried out properly.

With reference to conquering the phobia of school attendance, it has been found that many school children who are not reading and writing as well as they should may be just too frightened to do any better.[8] As mentioned in Chapter 4, otherwise "normal" children have phobias of certain school subjects, as other people irrationally fear heights or the sight of blood.

Many of the phobias connected with reading and writing result from conditioned reactions. After a time, the original problem may be resolved, but the barrier to learning which was removed has been replaced by another one, the phobia. Since the child could not read or write well, he was probably a failure in school. Children may associate reading and writing with failure and most of them are afraid of failing. In time, the fear can grow and the

---

[8]Walker, C. Eugene, "Phobias Hamper School Children," *Oklahoma Journal,* June 6, 1977.

child really needs help. It has been demonstrated that this help almost always comes by systematically desensitizing the fear.

Although systematic desensitization has proved to be a very successful procedure to use to desensitize children to fear, its use as a "self" administering device is not always applicable for fairly obvious reasons. This means that the child does not make up his or her own hierarchy of anxiety-evoking stimuli, but on the other hand, this is done by an adult, sometimes in collaboration with the child.

Although some fears are serious enough to warrant clinical intervention by a professional therapist, in many instances an "untrained" adult can be successful in the use of systematic desensitization with children. As a matter of fact, parents, without even being aware of it, sometimes actually practice systematic desensitization with their children. Take for example the first trip to the beach—a child may have a fear not only of the water but of the noise and vastness of the environment as well. A parent may desensitize the child's fear by unknowningly practicing the following hierarchy of anxiety-evoking stimuli. The child, accompanied by the parent, may play near the water for a time. Next, one foot is placed in the water, followed by both feet immersed to the ankles, then to the thighs, waist and finally immersion up to the neck.

Another example where a parent may unwittingly practice systematic desensitization with a child is when there is fear of the dark. The child may be permitted to sleep with a light on in his room for several nights, This is followed by turning out the light in the child's room but leaving one on in a nearby room with the door left open. On successive nights the door is closed more and more until the fear is eliminated and the child is encouraged to sleep with the light off and the door closed.

## Some Things to Consider
## When Using Systematic Desensitization with Children

If systematic desensitization is to meet with success when applied to children, there are certain considerations that need to be taken into account by adults. Most of these concerns center around the level of cognitive development of the child. In this regard, we have already mentioned the responsibility an adult should take in developing the hierarchy of anxiety-evoking stimuli.

Another cognitive factor to consider is the extent to which a child can apply his imagination to the stress-invoking scenes implied in the hierarchy of anxiety-evoking stimuli. In this particular regard, the late Jean Piaget, the world famous child development specialist, felt that developmentally imagery is thought to first occur in late infancy when "deferred imitation" takes place.[9] Mental imagery apparently cannot occur before this time. In "deferred imitation" the child is able to distinguish a mental image from the actual event it represents. However, Piaget felt that the image is very specific to the event it is imitating and is concrete rather than conceptual. Therefore, it is questionable whether four or five year old children can manipulate imagery in the ways required for systematic desensitization. It has also been suggested that the younger child may be able to attend to only a limited number of characteristics of the stimulus because of his or her stage of development.[10]

It could be that using such procedures in place of imagining scenes may be best for these children. For example, in what is called "in-vivo" desensitization, the child can use toys to play out a hierarchy of fear situations; or, the child can be allowed to draw the feared scenes.

In this general connection, the following series of steps involving a child's fear of birds is recommended by Barbara Kuczen.[11]

**Step 1.** Determine exactly what is fearful to the child. Encourage the child to talk about and explore the cause and nature of the problem. Do not take the fear lightly, ridicule, attempt coercion ("Don't be afraid, touch the birdie"), or ignore the problem. Logical explanation can help, but do not expect to explain away the fear.

---

[9]Piaget, Jean, *Les Mecanismes Perceptifs*, Paris, Presses Universitares de France, 1961.

[10]Bruner, J., Image and Symbol in Development of Magnitude and Order, In *The Causes of Behavior: Readings in Child Development and Educational Psychology*, Eds., J. F. Rosenblits and W. Allinsmith, Boston, Allyn & Bacon, Inc., 1969.

[11]Kuczen, Barbara, *Childhood Stress, Don't Let Your Child be a Victim*, New York, Delacorte Press, 1982, p. 149.

**Step 2.** If possible, arrange for the child to see others happy and safe in the situation he or she fears.

**Step 3.** Arrange for carefully supervised contact with the fear, during which you provide positive support and understanding. This procedure involves desensitization and might work as follows;

   a. Look at pictures of birds. Discuss whether or not a bird could actually harm you.
   b. Have the child hold a toy bird of some type, a plastic model, for example, or a stuffed animal.
   c. Let the child watch a friend caring for and holding a pet parrakeet. (Take care that the bird is a gentle one.)
   d. Have the child watch the parrakeet in its cage.
   e. Tell the child to touch the parrakeet briefly as the friend holds it.
   f. Have the child hold the parrakeet for five seconds with a pair of gloves on.
   g. Have the child hold the parrakeet for ten seconds with a pair of gloves on.
   h. Have the child hold the parrakeet for five seconds with bare hands.
   i. Have the child hold the parrakeet for ten seconds with bare hands.
   j. Have the child hold the parrakeet in lap and pet it.

What is called "anticipatory imagery" develops around age seven or eight. The imagery allows for manipulation of the mental representation so that it can be moved about in space or changed in form. It is plausible that seven and eight year olds could use systematic desensitization effectively. However, not too many studies using traditional systematic desensitization have been done with children under ten years of age. With many children, reinforcement may also be necessary to motivate the child to attempt and then practice visualizing.[12]

It is important to recognize that some authorities contend that the concrete images used by children below age seven or eight

---

[12]Whitehead, D'Ann, Shirley, Mariela and Walker, C. Eugene, Use of Systematic Desensitization in the Treatment of Children's Fears, In *Stress in Childhood* Ed., James H. Humphrey, New York, AMS Press, Inc., 1984, p. 220.

have a very high degree of affect associated with them. This means that there should be caution in the use of imagery of an aversive nature, due to the possibility that the child might imagine such an aversive scene and experience further trauma rather than alleviation of the fear.[13]

Another factor to take into account when using systematic desensitization with children is the extent to which they are able to learn relaxation techniques, as well as whether they are capable of relaxing in a short period of time. Of course, if relaxation procedures are presented to children in the same manner as they are for adults, they will have difficulty in learning how to relax. In our own work, we have never encountered this problem since our techniques for use of relaxation with children have always met with success. (These procedures are presented in detail in the following two chapters.)

In those cases where adults do have difficulty getting children to relax, a technique called "emotive imagery" has been used with success for many years. This technique replaces relaxation as the anxiety inhibiting response in systematic desensitization. It is meant to arouse feelings of bravery, pride, and assertiveness in the child. Like systematic desensitization a graduated hierarchy of the child's fears is developed. However, instead of imagining the scene concurrent with relaxing, the child is guided by the adult in imagery of the feared scene with credible events woven around a favorite hero. This could be one of the muppets, a cartoon character or a television hero.[14]

In summary, it should be luminously clear that when a given procedure can be used satisfactorily with adults, it does not follow automatically that it will be successful with children if used in the same way. Therefore, adults should exercise judgment and caution when making application of systematic desensitization with children.

---

[13]Elliott, C. H., and Ozolins, M., Use of Imagery and Imagination in Treatment of Children, In *Handbook of Child Clinical Psychology,* Eds. C. E. Walker and M. Roberts, New York, John Wiley & Sons, 1983.

[14]Lazarus, A. A. and Abramovitz, A., "The Use of Emotive Therapy in the Treatment of Children's Phobias," *Journal of Mental Science,* 1962, 108: 191–195.

# CHAPTER 8

# CONTROLLING STRESS
# THROUGH RELAXATION

M ost of us, children as well as adults, need some sort of relaxation in order to relieve the tensions encountered in daily living. The purpose of this chapter is to explore various facets of relaxation, along with those kinds of conditions that tend to produce a relaxed state. Emphasis will be placed on how adults themselves can learn to relax, and just as important how they can help children learn and develop techniques that will effectively influence their ability to relax.

## THE MEANING OF RELAXATION

One derivation of the term *relax* is from the Latin word *relaxare* meaning "loosen." It is interesting that a rather common parting comment among some people is the admonishment to "stay loose" — unquestionably good advice.

The reality of muscle fibers is that they have a response repertoire of one. All they can do is contract and this is the response they make to the electrochemical stimulation of impulses carried via the motor nerves. *Relaxation* is the removal of this stimulation.[1]

A relatively new term, *relaxation response*, has been coined by Herbert Benson.[2] This involves a number of bodily changes that occur in the organism when one experiences deep muscle relaxation. There is a response against "overstress," which brings on these bodily changes and brings the body back into what is a healthier

---

[1]Brown, Barbara B., *Stress and the Art of Biofeedback*, New York, Bantam Books, Inc., 1978, p. 31.

[2]Benson, Herbert, *The Relaxation Response*, New York, William Morrow and Company, Inc., 1975.

balance. Thus, the purpose of any kind of relaxation technique should be to induce a relaxation response.

From the point of view of the physiologist, relaxation is sometimes considered as "zero activity," or as nearly zero as one can manage in the neuromuscular system. That is, it is a neuromuscular accomplishment that results in reduction, or possible complete absence of muscle tone in a part of, or in, the entire body. It has been suggested that a primary value of relaxation lies in the lowering of brain and spinal cord activity, resulting from a reduction of nerve impulses, arising in muscle spindles and other sense endings in muscles, tendons, and joint structures.

The terms *relaxation, refreshment,* and *recreation* are often confused in their meaning. While all of these factors are important to the well-being of the human organism, they should not be used interchangeably to mean the same thing. *Refreshment* is the result of an improved blood supply to the brain for "refreshment" from central fatigue and to the muscles for the disposition of their waste products. This explains in part why mild muscular activity is good for overcoming the fatigue of sitting (seventh inning stretch) and for hastening recovery after strenuous exercise (an athlete continuing running a short distance slowly after a race).

*Recreation* may be described as the experience from which a person emerges with the feeling of being "re-created." No single activity is sure to bring this experience to all members of a group, nor is there assurance that an activity will provide recreation again for a given person because it did so the last time. These are more the marks of a psychological than a physiological experience. An important essential requirement for a recreational activity is that it completely engross the individual; that is, it must engage his or her undivided attention. It is really escape from the disintegrating effects of distraction to the healing effect of totally integrated activity. Experiences that produce this effect may range from a hard game of tennis to the reading of a comic strip.[3]

Some individuals consider recreation and relaxation to be one and the same thing, which is not the case. Recreation can be

---

[3]Steinhaus, Arthur, *Toward an Understanding of Health and Physical Education,* Dubuque, Iowa, Wm. C. Brown Publishers, 1963, p. 73.

considered a type of mental diversion that can be helpful in relieving tension. While mental and muscular tensions are inter-related, it is in the muscle that the tension state is manifested.

## LEARNING TO RELAX

For many years, recommendations have been made with regard to procedures individuals might apply in an effort to relax. Examples of some of these procedures are submitted in the ensuing discussions. In consideration of any technique designed to accomplish relaxation, one very important factor that needs to be taken into account is that learning to relax is a skill. That is, it is a skill based on the kinesthetic awareness of feelings of *tonus* (the normal degree of contraction present in most muscles, which keeps them always ready to function when needed). Unfortunately, it is a skill that very few of us practice—probably because we have little awareness of how to go about it.

One of the first steps in learning to relax is to experience tension. That is, one should be sensitive to tensions that exist in his or her body. This can be accomplished by voluntarily contracting a given muscle group, first very strongly and then less and less. Emphasis should be placed on detecting the signal of tension as the first step in "letting go"—(relaxing).

You might wish to try the traditional experiment used to demonstrate this phenomenon. Raise one arm so that the palm of the hand is facing outward away from your face. Now, bend the wrist backward and try to point the fingers back toward your face and down toward the forearm. You should feel some *strain* at the wrist joint. You should also feel something else in the muscle and this is tension, which is due to the muscle contracting the hand backward. Now, flop the hand forward with the fingers pointing downward and you will have accomplished a *tension-relaxation* cycle.

As in the case of any muscular skill, learning how to relax takes time and one should not expect to achieve complete satisfaction immediately. After one has identified a relaxation technique that he or she feels comfortable with, increased practice should eventually achieve satisfactory results.

## PROGRESSIVE RELAXATION FOR ADULTS

The technique of progressive relaxation was developed by Edmund Jacobson many years ago. It is still the technique most often referred to in the literature and probably the one that has had the most widespread application. In this technique, the person concentrates on progressively relaxing one muscle group after another. The technique is based on the procedure of comparing the difference between tension and relaxation. That is, as previously mentioned, one senses the feeling of tension in order to get the feeling of relaxation.

As mentioned previously, learning to relax is a skill that you can develop in applying the principles of progressive relaxation. One of the first steps is to be able to identify the various muscle groups and how to tense them so that tension and relaxation can be experienced. However, before we make suggestions on how to tense and relax the various muscle groups, there are certain preliminary measures that need to be taken into account.

1. You must understand that this procedure takes time and like anything else, the more you practice, the more proficient you should become with the skills.
2. Progressive relaxation is not the kind of thing to be done spontaneously, and you should be prepared to spend from 20 to 30 minutes daily in tensing-relaxing activities.
3. The particular time of day is important and this is pretty much an individual matter. Some recommendations suggest that progressive relaxation be practiced daily; sometime during the day and again in the evening before retiring. For many people, this would be difficult unless one time period was set aside before going to the job or to school in the morning. This might be a good possibility and might help a person to start the day relaxed.
4. It is important to find a suitable place to practice the tensing-relaxing activities. Again this is an individual matter with some preferring a bed or couch and others a comfortable chair.
5. Consideration should be given to the amount of time a given

muscle is tensed. You should be sure that you are able to feel the difference between tension and relaxation. This means that tension should be maintained from about four to not more than eight seconds.

6. Another important point to take into account is what sort of "mental practice," if any, should be used as the muscles are tensed and relaxed. In this connection, some clinical psychologists may use mental practice predominantly, as in the case suggested later in the chapter.

7. Breathing is an important concomitant in tensing and relaxing muscles. To begin with, it is suggested that three or more deep breaths be taken and held for about five seconds. This will tend to make for better rhythm in breathing. Controlled breathing makes it easier to relax and it is most effective when it is done deeply and slowly. It is ordinarily recommended that one should inhale deeply when the muscles are tensed and exhale slowly when "letting go."

## How to Tense and Relax Various Muscle Groups

Muscle groups may be identified in different ways. The classification given here consists of four different groups: (1) muscles of the head, face, tongue, and neck; (2) muscles of the trunk; (3) muscles of the upper extremities; and (4) muscles of the lower extremities.

### Muscles of the Head, Face, Tongue, and Neck

There are two chief muscles of the head, the one covering the back of the head and the one covering the front of the skull. There are about 30 muscles of the face, including muscles of the orbit and eyelids, mastication, lips, tongue, and neck. Incidentally, it has been estimated that it takes 26 facial muscles to frown and a proportionately much smaller number to smile.

Muscles of this group may be tensed and relaxed as follows (relaxation is accomplished by "letting go" after tensing).

1. Raise your eyebrows by opening the eyes as wide as possible. You might wish to look into a mirror to see if you have formed wrinkles on the forehead.

2. Tense the muscles on either side of your nose like you were going to sneeze.
3. Dilate or flare out the nostrils.
4. Force an extended smile from "ear to ear" at the same time clenching your teeth.
5. Pull one corner of your mouth up and then the other up as in a "villainous sneer."
6. Draw your chin up as close to your chest as possible.
7. Do the opposite of the above trying to draw your head back as close to your back as possible.

### Muscles of the Trunk

Included in this group are the muscles of the back, chest, abdomen, and pelvis. Here are some ways you can tense some of these muscles.

1. Bring your chest forward and at the same time put your shoulders back with emphasis on bringing your shoulder blades as close together as possible.
2. Try to round your shoulders and bring your shoulder blades far apart. This is pretty much the opposite of the above.
3. Give your shoulders a shrug, trying to bring them up to your ears, at the same time as you try to bring your neck downward.
4. Breathe deeply, and hold it momentarily, and then blow out the air from your lungs rapidly.
5. Draw in your stomach so that your chest is out beyond your stomach. Exert your stomach muscles by forcing out to make it look like you are fatter than you are.

### Muscles of the Upper Extremities

This group includes muscles of the hands, forearms, upper arms, and shoulders. A number of muscles situated in the trunk may be grouped with the muscles of the upper extremities, their function being to attach the upper limbs to the trunk and move the shoulders and arms. In view of this, there is some overlapping in muscle groups *two* and *three*. Following are some ways to tense some of these muscles.

1. Clench the fist and then open the hand, extending the fingers as far as possible.
2. Raise one arm shoulder high and parallel to the floor. Bend at the elbow and bring the hand in toward the shoulder. Try to touch your shoulders while attempting to move the shoulder away from the hand. Flex your opposite biceps in the same manner.
3. Stretch one arm out to the side of the body and try to point the fingers backward toward the body. Do the same with the other arm.
4. Hold the arm out the same way as above but this time have the palm facing up and point the fingers inward toward the body. Do the same with the other arm.
5. Stretch one arm out to the side, clench the fist and roll the wrist around slowly. Do the same with the other arm.

**Muscles of the Lower Extremities**

This group includes muscles of the hips, thighs, legs, feet, and buttocks. Following are ways to tense some of these muscles.

1. Hold one leg out straight and point your toes as far forward as you can. Do the same with the other leg.
2. Do the same as above but point your toes as far backward as you can.
3. Turn each foot outward as far as you can and release. Do just the opposite by turning the foot inward as far as you can.
4. Try to draw the thigh muscles up so that you can see the form of the muscles.
5. Make your buttocks tense by pushing down if you are sitting in a chair. If you are lying down try to draw the muscles of the buttocks in close by attempting to force the cheeks together.

The above suggestions include several possibilities for tensing various muscles of the body. As you practice some of these, you will also discover other ways to tense and then let go. A word of caution might be that, in the early stages, you should be alert to the possibility of cramping certain muscles. This can happen particularly with those muscles that are not frequently used. This means that at the beginning you should proceed carefully. It might be a good idea to keep a record or diary of your sessions so that you can refer back to these experiences if this might be necessary. This will also help you get into each new session by reviewing your experiences in previous sessions.

## MENTAL PRACTICE AND IMAGERY IN RELAXATION FOR ADULTS

**Mental practice** is a symbolized rehearsal of a physical activity in the absence of any gross muscular movement. This means that a person imagines in his own mind the way he will perform a given activity. *Imagery* is concerned with the development of a mental image that may aid one in the performance of an activity. In mental practice, the person thinks through what he is going to do, and with imagery he may suggest to himself, or another may suggest a condition to him, and he then tries to effect a mental image of the condition.

The use of mental practice in performing motor skills is not new. In fact, research in this general area has been going on for well over half a century. This research has revealed that imagining a movement will likely produce recordable electric action potentials emanating from the muscle groups that would be called up if the movement were to be actually carried out. In addition, most mental activity is accompanied by general rises in muscular tension.

One procedure in the use of mental practice for relaxation is that of making suggestions to one's self. For the most part, in early childhood, we first learn to act on the basis of verbal instructions from others. Later we learn to guide and direct our own behavior on the basis of our own language activities—we literally talk to ourselves, giving ourselves instructions. This point of view has long been supported by research that postulates that speech as a form of communication between children and adults later becomes a means of organizing the child's own behavior. That is, the function that was previously divided between two people—child and adult—becomes an internal function of human behavior.

An example is an approach recommended by C. Eugene Walker[4] involving one making relaxation-connected statements to himself or herself. He suggests the following specific illustration.

> I am going to relax completely. First I will relax my forehead and scalp. I will let all the muscles of my forehead and scalp relax and become completely at rest. All of the wrinkles will come out of my forehead and that part of my body will relax completely. Now, I will relax the muscles of my face. I will just let them relax and go limp. There will be no tension in my jaw. Next, I will relax my neck muscles. Just let them become tranquil and allow all the pressure to leave them. My neck muscles are relaxing completely. Now, I will relax the muscles of my shoulders. That relaxation will spread down my arms to the elbows, down the forearm to wrists, hands and fingers. My arms will just dangle from the frame of my body. I will now relax the muscles of my chest. I will let them relax. I will take a deep breath and relax, letting all the tightness and tenseness leave. My breathing will now be normal and relaxed, and I will relax the muscles of my stomach. Now, I will relax all the muscles up and down both sides of the spine; now, the waist, buttocks, and thighs down to my knees. Now, the relaxation will spread to the calves of my legs, ankles, feet, and toes. I will just lie here and continue to let all the muscles go completely limp. I will become completely relaxed from the top of my head to the tips of my toes.

## USING RELAXATION WITH CHILDREN

Until relatively recent years, the use of relaxation as a means of controlling stress appears to have been reserved only for adults. However, in more modern times relaxation procedures have been found to be very effective with children. Moreover, there is some objective evidence to support the idea that the practice of relaxation with children can be beneficial to them in various ways. For example, one study found that there could be significant changes in attentiveness of school children when relaxation training was used.[5] Various other studies have have shown that certain measures of anxiety can be lowered as a result of the use of relaxation

[4]Walker, C. Eugene, *Learn to Relax, 13 Ways to Reduce Tension*, Englewood Cliffs, New Jersey, Prentice-Hall, Inc., 1975, p. 10.

[5]Bednarova, N., An Investigation Concerning the Influence of Psychotonic Exercises Upon the Indices of Concentration of Attentiveness, *Teor. Prax. Teles. Vychon*, 16(4), 101–111.

procedures.[6,7] It has also been found that there is improvement in self-help skills of retarded children after relaxation exercises.[8]

The relaxation techniques used with children follow the same theory of relaxation used with adults; that is, the purpose is to experience tension in a muscle or group of muscles and then "let go." As we shall see later, some practices with children differ from those used with adults since an effort is ordinarily made to make it more of a "fun" experience for children. In addition, some form of imagery is almost always used with children while this practice is more or less optional with adults.

## Progressive Relaxation for Children

Although progressive relaxation is likely to be most useful for adults, with certain variations it can be used successfully with children. One good way that we have found to use it with children is by playing the game of "Mirrors." The adult takes a position opposite the child (or several children) and asks the child to imitate what he or she (the adult) does. That is, the child "mirrors" the adult's performance.

Others have used progressive relaxation successfully with children as well. For example, two of our collaborators on a childhood stress project, Psychologists John Carter and Harold Russel[9] have developed a series of tapes for child relaxation. One of these is patterned after the idea of progressive relaxation, and involves tensing and relaxing various muscle groups. This is to help make the children aware of their own muscular tension and to learn how it feels to release their tensions. In the following sequence chil-

---

[6]Johnson, D. I., and Spielberger, C. D., The Effects of Relaxation Training and Passage of Time on Measures of Static and Trait Anxiety, *Journal of Clinical Psychology,* 24(1), 20–23.

[7]Keat, D. B., Broad Spectrum Behavior Therapy with Children: A Case Presentation, *Behavior Therapy,* 3(1), 169–174.

[8]Cratty, Bryant J., *Physical Expressions of Intelligence,* Englewood Cliffs, New Jersey, Prentice-Hall, Inc., 1972, p. 113.

[9]Carter, John L. and Russel, Harold, Use of Biofeedback Relaxation Procedures with Learning Disabled Children, In *Stress in Childhood,* Ed. James H. Humphrey, New York, AMS Press, Inc., 1984, p. 286.

dren are asked to tense for five seconds and then to relax and feel
the tension leaving for ten seconds.

1. Squeeze your eyes shut—tightly—hold it, relax.
2. Push your lips together, very tightly—hold it, relax.
3. Press your tongue to the roof of your mouth—hold it—relax.
4. Shrug your shoulders up toward your ears—hold it—relax—
   feel the tension leaving.
5. With both hands make a fist as tight as you can—feel the
   tension building—relax. Feel the tension leaving.
6. Make a fist with your right hand. Notice the difference
   between your tense right hand and your relaxed left. Relax
   your right hand.
7. Make a fist with your left hand. Feel the left hand getting
   tense while your right hand is relaxing—relax your left
   hand.
8. Pull your stomach way in toward your backbone—hold
   it—relax—feel the tension leaving.
9. Push your knees together—hard—hold it. Relax.
10. Pull your toes toward your knees, way up. Hold it, hold it,
    relax. Feel the tensions leaving your legs.
11. Point your toes. Hold it—relax.
12. Now tighten every muscle in your body—hold it—relax
    your entire body. Let your entire body get very limp—relaxed
    and comfortable.

When this is completed, breathing instructions are presented.
The children are asked to breathe in through their nose and out
through their mouth. They are asked to do this naturally and
rhythmically. Each time they breathe out, they are reminded to let
themselves get just a little more limp, a little more relaxed, and a
little more comfortable.

And finally, Harry Krampf and his associates report success
with what they call *guided progressive sessions* as a part of a Summer
Youth Fitness School for children ages seven to fourteen.[10] They
used a series of guided progressive sessions to assist the partici-

[10]Krampf, Harry, Hopkins, Dave, and Bird, John, "Muscular Relaxation for the Elementary School Student," *Journal of Physical Education and Recreation*, April, 1979.

pants in becoming aware of their tensions and how to release these tensions. In this format, there are four component parts: (1) relaxation of individual muscles, (2) relaxation of groups of muscles, (3) relaxation of principal muscle groups, and (4) relaxation of the total body. It is suggested that the practice setting be conducive to relaxation, and this includes a comfortable room temperature, loose-fitting clothing, lighting that is not too bright, and the provision of a soft surface such as mats. The first step involves practice of controlled breathing followed by helping children to realize the difference between being tense and limp. The next step is to use the tensing-releasing procedure, progressing through the various body parts.

## Using Imagery in Relaxation for Children

In discussing the use of imagery in relaxation with children, we need to make the differentiation between its use with systematic desensitization. With regard to the latter, we have already said that it is a problem for some children to imagine the scenes in a hierarchy of anxiety-evoking stimuli. A reason for this is the preciseness of such scenes because a child is given little latitude in "letting his mind wander." On the contrary, as we shall see later, using imagery in relaxation gives the child an opportunity to visualize and enjoy a situation by creating his own image of it. In addition, use of imagery in relaxation is a joyful experience while in systematic desensitization the child is asked to imagine scenes that provoke anxiety.

A number of research studies report success in using imagery as an aspect of relaxation with children. One study[11] used imagery to advantage on self-instructional training with hyperactive and impulsive children. In another study[12] there was success with imagery in the development of a self-control program. A technique was developed to train disruptive children to have control by pairing imagery and relaxation.

---

[11]Kanfer, F., and Goldstein, A. P., *Helping People Change: A Textbook of Methods*, New York, The Pergamon Press, 1975.

[12]Schneider, M., and Robin, A., *Turtle Manual*, Stony Brook, New York, Psychology Department, State University of New York, 1974.

In what he termed the "release only" phase of relaxation, Robert McBrien[13] used instructions involving imagery as follows:

> Just imagine you are lying on your back on soft green grass—you are so comfortable as you look up through the branches and leaves of a shade tree at the deep blue sky—you can see soft white puffy clouds floating by. (Further instructions to focus on the pleasant feeling of relaxation would then follow.)

Another way imagery can be used to promote a relaxed state is by making short comparative statements to children such as "float like a feather" or "melt like ice." In this regard, we have prepared several stories which can be used for this purpose—two of which are reproduced here.[14] The adult reads the story to the child, and then with various degrees of adult guidance, the child tries to depict the activity in the reading selection by creating his own responses and helping himself to relax.

### SNOWFLAKES

Snow!
Snowflakes fall.
They fall down.
Down, down, down.
Around and around.
Could you move like snowflakes?

### MR. SNOWMAN AND MR. SUN

See Mr. Snowman.
See Mr. Sun.
Mr. Snowman sees Mr. Sun.
Mr. Snowman is going.
Going, going, going.
Mr. Snowman is gone.
Be Mr. Snowman.

The previously-mentioned John Carter and Harold Russel have prepared another tape called "Float Ride" which focuses on visual imagery. The following narrative is presented in a soft, slow and

---

[13]McBrien, Robert J., "Using Relaxation Methods with First Grade Boys," *Elementary School Guidance and Counseling,* February, 1978.

[14]For additional stories see: Humphrey, James H., and Humphrey, Joy N., *Help Your Child Learn the 3R's Through Active Play,* Springfield, Illinois, Charles C Thomas, Publisher, 1980.

soothing voice, giving children plenty of time to listen, absorb and passively follow the directions. The dashes represent pauses. Soft music is in the background.

## FLOAT RIDE

Now, get in a very comfortable position _____

Close your eyes, and try to relax your body _____

Think about your breathing _____

Breathe in _____ Breathe out _____

Breathe in through your nose, and out through your mouth _____

Now take a deep breath, hold it _____

Let it out slowly _____

Feel yourself sinking deeper and deeper into the chair _____

You're beginning to feel very comfortable and relaxed _____

Today we're going to take a ride on a float in the Gulf. We each have a float and it needs to be blown up _____

So first thing we do is blow them up. Take your float and blow into it, by taking deep breaths and exhaling into the float _____

You will need to blow into your float at least ten times _____

So now, take a very deep breath and, slowly exhale into your float _____

Each time you breathe out, let your body become more and more relaxed _____

Each breath should let you feel really good inside _____

Now that our floats are blown up, we'll walk down to the water.

The sun is very bright and it feels warm on your skin _____

The sand feels warm and cushy and soft against our feet _____

As we get closer to the water we can smell the salty air _____

We can hear the waves _____ of the ocean as they hit the beach __

The water is closer now and the sand begins to get a little cooler _____

The sun is shining on us, and we feel good _____

We will pause for a few moments now to feel the sun and the sand beneath our feet _____

We are now at the edge of the water and we get on our floats _____

The floats feel very comfortable and secure _____

The air is warm and the water is cool _____

We are slowly floating away from the shore on our floats and we feel very relaxed _____

There are seagulls in the sky and we open our eyes to watch them fly by us _____

The water is warm and we feel it with our hands and our legs _____

The water is moving our floats away from the beach and we feel very comfortable and safe _____

As the waves pass under us, the floats move slowly up, and slowly down __

We move with the floats _____ up, and down _____ up, and down _____ very slowly _____

We feel as if we were being rocked to sleep _____

The water is pushing us up and down _____ up, and down _____

We feel very relaxed and comfortable _____

As the waves are passing under us, they begin to pull us closer and closer to the beach _____

For just a few more seconds we can ride on our float without having to touch the sand _____

The sun is warming our bodies, and the float ride is relaxing our bodies and our minds _____

The floats touch the sand and we must get our bodies to move again _____

So for a few seconds, bring yourself back to alertness and get off the float __

The sand feels warm against our feet once more and we feel very good inside and outside _____

The air is warm and is drying our bodies quickly as we slowly walk away from the water _____

Now we let the air out of the floats, and with each gust of wind escaping from the float we let it relax our bodies _____

Now we have finished with the ride and with the floats and must return to the room _____

As I count backward from five to one, slowly bring yourself back to being alert and relaxed _____

5 _____

4 _____ Begin to feel more alert and allow energy to flow into your body _____

3 _____ Move your arms and legs _____

2 _____ Wiggle your fingers and your toes _____ open your eyes.

1 _____ Sit up, stretch and feel alert and good all over.

## Relaxation Games

An example of the successful use of the game format in providing for relaxation in children is one suggested by the aforementioned Robert McBrien. He used this approach in the tensing releasing phase with the game *Simon Says*. Each muscle group to be tensed and then relaxed is prefaced by "Simon Says," that is, "Simon says to close your eyes...Simon says to make your eyebrows touch your hair...Simon says to let go and feel your eyes relax." A five-second tensing of any muscle is followed by 15 seconds of releasing the muscle. The sequence for relaxing the muscles prefaced by "Simon Says" follows:

1. Head
   a. Try to make your eyebrows touch your hair.
   b. Squeeze your eyes shut.
   c. Wrinkle up your nose.
   d. Press your lips together.
   e. Press your tongue against the roof of your mouth.
2. Shoulders and back
   a. Lift your shoulders, and try to touch your ears.
   b. Bring your shoulders back as far as they will go.
3. Hands and arms
   a. Make your fist as tight as you can.
   b. Show me your arm muscles.
4. Stomach—Make your stomach as hard as you can; pull it way in.
5. Upper legs
   a. Lift your legs and feet off the floor.
   b. Press your knees together.
6. Lower legs and feet
   a. Press your ankles together.
   b. Press your feet together.

**Note:** The game Simon Says is played as follows: One or more children face the person who plays Simon. Every time Simon says to do something, the children do it; however, if a command is given without the prefix "Simon says," the child or children remain motionless. For example, when the leader issues the command "Simon says press your ankles together," this is done, but if the leader just says "Press your knees together," the command is not executed.

In the following chapter where creative movement is used to help children accomplish relaxation, many of the activities are performed in a game-like manner.

# CHAPTER 9

# CONTROLLING STRESS
# THROUGH CREATIVE MOVEMENT

In order to provide the reader with an understanding of its
meaning, it is appropriate to give a literal description of *creative
movement*. The word *creative* means "to bring into existence." The
term *movement*, when applied to the human body, simply means a
"change in body position." Therefore, when we put the two words
creative and movement together, the interpretation is bringing
something into existence by expressing one's self by means of
body movement. This creative action can pertain to the whole
body or various body parts, and, as we shall see later, this procedure is basic to creative relaxation as a means of stress reduction in
children.

## CREATIVITY AND CHILDHOOD

One of the utmost concerns in our modern democratic society is
the problem of how to provide for creative expression so that a
child may develop to the fullest extent. Democracy is only beginning to understand the power of the individual as perhaps the
most dynamic force in the world today. It is in this frame of
reference that creativity should come clearly into focus, because
many of the problems in our complex society can be solved
mainly through creative thinking.

Creative experience involves *self*-expression. It is concerned
with the need to experiment, to express original ideas, and to
think. Creativity and childhood have a natural relationship because
children are naturally creative. They imagine. They pretend.
They are uninhibited. They are not only original, but actually
ingenious in their thoughts and actions. Indeed, creativity is a

characteristic inherent in the lives of practically all children. It may range from some children who create as a natural form of expression without adult stimulation, to others who may need varying degrees of adult guidance and encouragement.

There are various means of creative expression, and art, music and writing are considered to be the traditional approaches. However, as far as children are concerned, the very essence of creative expression is movement. It is a form of creativity that uses the body as the instrument of expression. For the young child, the most *natural* form of creative expression is movement. Because of their very nature, children have an inclination for movement, and they use this medium as the basic form of creative expression. Movement is the child's universal language, a most important form of communication and a most meaningful way of learning.

## CREATIVE RELAXATION

There are at least two different versions of what can be termed *creative relaxation*. In his interesting book, *High Level Wellness,* Donald B. Ardell[1] considers it to be an awakening of different parts of the breathing body, a gentle way of reaching the flow of vital energy deep within where experience and creativity penetrate each other. The approach to creative relaxation presented here was developed by the second author of this book for the purpose of reducing stress in young children. It combines a form of imagery and tensing and releasing which the reader should recall was discussed in the preceding chapter. A child or a group of children with various degrees of adult guidance, creates a movement(s) designed to tense and relax individual muscles, muscle groups or the entire body. The procedure is applicable in the home to be used by parents as well as applicable in the school setting to be used by teachers. In addition, it can be applied in camp situations, particularly as a remedy for homesickness.

Creative relaxation simply means that there are contrasting creative movements that give the effect of tensing and letting go. An illustration is provided here for a better understanding of it.

---

[2]Ardell, Donald B., *High Level Wellness,* New York, Bantam Books, Inc. 1979, p. 44.

This example shows the contrast (tensing and letting go) of the muscles of the arm. The leader could start by raising a question such as the following:

"What would you say is the main difference between a ball bat and a jump rope?"

This question is then discussed and will no doubt lead to the major difference, being that a ball bat is hard and stiff, and that a jump rope is soft and limp. The leader might then proceed as follows:

"Let's see if we can all make one of our arms be like a ball bat." (This movement is created.) "Now, quickly, can you make your arm be like a jump rope? (The movement is created by releasing the tensed arm.) *Note: The length of time for tensing should be four to six seconds.*

The experience can then be evaluated by using such questions as:

"How did your arm feel when you made it like a bat?"
"How did your arm feel when you made it like a jump rope?"

The creative leader can produce a discussion that will increase an understanding of relaxation. This is but one example and others will be presented in the following discussion.

## CREATIVE MOVEMENTS FOR
## GENERAL AND SPECIFIC RELAXATION

For our purposes *general* relaxation involves the entire body, and *specific* relaxation is concerned with an individual muscle or a group of muscles. Specific relaxation as used here should not be confused with what some persons call *differential* relaxation. Those who use this term generally consider it to be concerned with relaxing all muscles except those that are actually needed for the particular occupation at hand.

In considering the examples of creative movement experiences that are recommended here, it appears important to make some general suggestions for their use. The following descriptive list is submitted for this purpose.

1. Because of their very nature, most creative movements tend to be relaxing. The reason for this is that they are conducted

in an informal atmosphere with a minimum amount of formal structuring.

2. Although most children are naturally creative, some will show evidence of more creativity than others. This means that, depending upon the nature of a particular creative experience, along with the creative level of the child, there is a need to determine the extent of adult guidance needed in each situation. With practice, most adult leaders will be able to make a judgment that is in the best interest of the children.

3. A very important aspect in conducting creative movement with children is the leader's voice. The manner in which a leader speaks, along with the intonation of certain words, can have a profound influence on children's creative responses. For example, a soft tone of voice tends to make children respond with a slower movement. A sharp or loud tone tends to cause children to respond more vigorously. Even the words can have an influence on children's responses. For instance, words like *hard* and *soft* and *heavy* and *light* are likely to inspire feelings and emotions that will result in varying responses. The important thing to keep uppermost in mind is that there should be contrasting experience—tensing and letting go. The voice can have a pronounced influence on this experience.

4. The format for conducting the various activities is intended only as a general way of organizing the experiences. For this reason, the suggested procedures should be considered as a guide and not necessarily as a prescription to be followed. In other words, individuals should inject their own creative ideas into the procedures for conducting the experiences. The suggested format consists of (a) the name of the activity, (b) suggested leader input, (c) some possible children's responses, and (d) suggested evaluation procedures.

5. The question of *where* to conduct the activities is important. Some can be conducted while sitting in a chair or on the surface area. Others may require more space. The nature of the activity itself will ordinarily indicate where the activity might best take place. One very important consideration in this regard is that, for those activities that suggest that the child might respond by falling to the surface area, a soft

landing surface should be provided for this purpose. This could be a rug or other suitable soft landing surface.

(*NOTE:* Creative movement responses of children are pretty much an individual matter; that is, each child is likely to respond in the way that the experience means to him personally. Therefore, a creative movement experience can be conducted with a group of children with each child creating his own more or less unique responses. At the same time, any of the suggested activities can be presented to a single child. Although the activities can be used with individual children or with groups of children, the indication in the descriptions of the activities is that they are for a group of children. When using the activities with one child, the format and procedures can easily be adjusted and modified for that purpose.)

### Examples of Creative Movements for General Relaxation

**Activity:**

**HARD AND SOFT.** A major purpose of this activity is to help children distinguish between the terms *hard* and *soft*. The opening discussion can be oriented in this direction.

**Introduction:**

The leader can ask the children if they know the difference between hard and soft.

**Responses:**

Children might respond by naming some things that are hard and soft. (If this does not happen, the leader can guide the discussion with certain questions.)

**Leader:**

Is a rock hard?
Is the pavement hard?
Can it be made soft?
(The purpose here is to help those children who do not know the difference, or how to explain the difference, to be able to

distinguish between hard and soft. All such questions will be governed by the original responses of the children.)

**Leader:**

We have talked about some of the things that are hard and some that are soft. I wonder if you could do something to make yourself hard?

**Responses:**

Children respond by creating shapes and positions that depict their bodies are being hard.

**Leader:**

Now, can you do something that will make your body feel soft?

**Responses:**

Children do several things that give them the feeling of a soft body.

**Leader:**

All right. Very good. I am going to say the word *hard,* and when you hear it, I want you to make yourself feel hard. After that, I will say the word *soft,* and then you make yourself feel soft. (The leader calls out the word *hard* and has the children hold their position for three or four seconds before calling out the word *soft.* The leader should take advantage of appropriate intonation of the words *hard* and *soft.*)

**Evaluation:**

A discussion can be developed with questions such as the following:

How did you feel when you were hard?

How did you feel when you were soft?

Did you feel better when you pretended you were hard or when you were soft?

Could you feel the difference?

**Activity:**

**COLD AND HOT.** In working with children in creative movement, it has been found that there are certain conditions that cause children to react more or less "naturally" to specific situations. The activity COLD AND HOT is a case in point. When children are asked to respond to *cold* they tend to react with a "tensed up" body condition. When responding to *hot* they tend to react with a more relaxed state. This is probably because children have had the actual experience of being cold and hot.

**Introduction:**

The leader can introduce the discussion by referring to certain climatic or seasonal conditions that will depict cold and hot. Some introductory questions could include the following:

Is a piece of ice hot or cold?

Is the sun hot or cold?

If you have been out on a cold winter day, how did it make you feel?

How does it feel to be out on a hot summer day?

Can you think of some things that are cold or hot?

(The leader attempts to guide the discussion in the direction of a person's feelings when the body is cold and/or hot.)

**Responses:**

Some children are likely to suggest that they shiver when cold and sweat when hot. Others will tell about their experiences with things that are hot and cold.

**Leader:**

You have told a lot of things about cold and hot. Now, how would you like to show us how it feels to be cold and how it feels to be hot? When I say the word *cold,* please show us what you would do with your body. When I say the word *hot,* show us what your body would do. (The leader continues with this procedure as the children create body movements that express hot and cold.)

**Evaluation:**

Did you feel "looser" when you were cold or when you were hot? George, you made your body into a ball when I said "Cold," and when I said "Hot," you flopped over and spread out your arms. Why did you do that? Could you tell us the different feeling you had when you pretended to be cold than when you pretended to be hot?

**Activity:**

**RAIN AND SNOW.** Although this activity is somewhat like the previous ones, it differs because it is likely to be an experience in which most children have participated on their own. Experience has shown that when children are asked to imitate rain, they tend to make their bodies tense. When imitating snow, they appear to relax the body. It could be speculated that the reason for this is that they generally associate rain as *heavy* and snow as *light*. The discussion could be guided in this particular direction.

**Introduction:**

One good way to introduce this activity is to ask the difference between rain and snow.

**Responses:**

Some typical responses are the following:
Rain is wetter than snow.
Rain comes down harder than snow.
Snow is white; rain does not have a color.
It is more fun playing in the snow than it is in the rain.
My mother doesn't care if I play in the snow, but she does not like to have me play in the rain.

**Leader:**

You have suggested some very interesting ways in which snow and rain are different. Now, how do you think it would make you feel to pretend you are rain—and then snow?

**Responses:**

Children express different feelings.

**Leader:**

You have told many different ways it could feel to be like rain and snow. Now, let's pretend we are one and then the other. I will say "Rain," and then I will say "Snow," (The leader alternates calling out "Rain" and "Snow" as the children try to create movements in the form of these elements.)

**Evaluation:**

Which did you like best — pretending you were rain or pretending you were snow?

How did it feel to be like rain?

How did it feel to be like snow?

When did it feel more restful — when you were rain or when you were snow?

Did you feel heavier when you were rain?

Did you feel lighter when you were snow?

Which one gave you the better feeling?

**Activity:**

**PEANUT BUTTER AND MILK.** This activity is similar to the preceding one because the substances (peanut butter and milk) are concerned with contrasting consistency. Peanut butter is thought of as a thick substance, while milk is thought of as a thin substance.

**Introduction:**

The discussion can be introduced by raising questions about the two foods as follows:

How many of you drink milk every day?

How many of you have eaten peanut butter?

What is the difference between the two?

What do you think would happen if we tried to pour peanut butter like we pour milk?

**Responses:**

Children generally respond in terms of the thickness of peanut butter and the thinness of milk. Typical responses are the following:

You don't spread milk like you spread peanut butter.

You can't make a sandwich out of milk.

You eat peanut butter, but you drink milk.

You can eat a peanut butter sandwich, and then drink milk.

**Leader:**

Those are all good ideas. Now, how do you think it would feel to make your body like peanut butter and then like milk? Let's try it. I will say "Peanut butter," and then I will say "Milk," and you try to change from one to the other.

**Evaluation:**

How did you feel when you made yourself like peanut butter?

How did you feel when you made yourself like milk?

Was it easier to make yourself like peanut butter or like milk?

Which was more fun?

**Activity:**

THE KITE. This activity is concerned with a kite in flight being kept up by the wind. This is compared to when the wind ceases and the kite begins to descend.

**Introduction:**

In the introductory discussion, the leader poses questions such as the following:

What is a kite?

How many of you have ever had a kite?

Did you ever try to make a kite?

How can you make a kite fly?

What makes a kite stay in the air?

What happens when a kite begins to fall?

**Responses:**

There will be many various responses, with the leader attempting to guide the discussion in the direction of the purpose of the activity.

**Leader:**

How do you think it would feel to be like a kite up in the air?

**Responses:**

Children express their feelings, and the leader encourages them to demonstrate. (Children will perform in many different ways with the most prevalent way being to take a forward leaning stance with arms outspread to the sides. This tends to cause the muscles of the body to become tense.)

**Leader:**

You are all very good at being a kite. Now, let's try being a kite in the air, kept up by the wind, and a kite after the wind stops blowing. When I say "Up," it will mean that you are a kite in the air, and when I say "Down," it will mean that the wind has stopped and the kite comes down.

**Evaluation:**

How did you feel when you were a kite in the air?
How did you feel when the wind stopped?
What was the difference in your body when you were a kite in the air and when you were a kite when the wind stopped?

**Activity:**

**THE BALLOON.** This activity involves a balloon being blown up to capacity and then the air suddenly being released. A very important feature of this activity is that it helps a child learn about controlled breathing, which is so important to muscular relaxation. This activity provides for rhythm in breathing as the child inhales deeply, then exhales, and becomes relaxed when the air is released from the balloon.

**Introduction:**

To begin the discussion, the leader can use questions such as the following:

Did you ever blow up a balloon and then let it go?

What happens if you blow it up too hard?

What happens when you let it go?

(It might be a good idea for the leader to start the discussion with a real balloon. It can be blown up and then let go with the questions and discussion from this point.)

**Responses:**

Children will provide many responses verbally, but many times they will immediately try to show what a balloon does when it is let go with air in it.

**Leader:**

Good! You are acting like you are a balloon. Now, let's blow up like a balloon, and when I say "let go," everyone do what a balloon would do when the air comes out.

**Evaluation:**

Did you feel tight when you took the air in like a balloon?

How did it make you feel when you were holding the air?

How did it make you feel when you let go?

Was it a better feeling to hold the air in or to let it go?

## Examples of Creative Movement for Specific Relaxation

The reader should notice that some of the activities for specific relaxation involved a certain degree of structuring. This means that children should still be free to explore various ways of performing an activity. At the same time, the leader should provide enough guidance in the creative response to direct the performance of an activity in a manner in which the objective of the activity will be reached.

## Muscles of the Head, Face, Tongue, and Neck

Children particularly enjoy activities in this muscle group because it gives them an opportunity to make "funny faces" legitimately.

### Activity:

BIG EYE. In this activity the eyes are opened as wide as possible for a period of about four to six seconds. Also, the person can look to the right, left, above, and below.

### Introduction:

The leader can name the activity and ask the children what they think it means.

### Responses:

Some children will immediately respond by opening their eyes very wide.

### Leader:

When I say "Big Eye," try to open your eyes wide and hold it until I say "Little Eye."

### Evaluation:

How did it feel to have a big eye?
Did it feel different to have a little eye?

### Activity:

THE SNEEZE. The muscles are contracted on either side of the nose as in sneezing. The skin should be wrinkled upward over the nose as hard as possible.

### Introduction:

The activity can be introduced by discussing how one looks when sneezing. There can also be a discussion of what causes one to sneeze.

**Responses:**

The children consider this to be a very funny activity, and they will respond in a variety of ways. Some will immediately try to do a forced sneeze.

**Leader:**

I want you to show how you would look when you are getting ready to sneeze. When I say "Ready," everyone pretend to get ready to sneeze. When I say "Sneeze," everyone pretend to sneeze.

**Evaluation:**

Did your face feel tight when you were getting ready to sneeze? How did your face feel after you pretended to sneeze?

**Activity:**

**THE FROWN.** There are many ways to perform this activity which include (1) stretching the left corner of the mouth up and out, (2) stretching the right corner of the mouth down and out, (3) stretching the left corner of the mouth down and out, and (4) stretching the lower lip down hard while trying to keep the lip flat.

**Introduction:**

A discussion can begin about smiling and frowning, with consideration of how they are alike and different, why people smile and frown, and what it means to keep a "straight" face. Also the leader can mention the different kinds of frowns suggested above.

**Responses:**

While children will respond verbally, more often than not, they will immediately respond by frowning and smiling.

**Leader:**

Let's play a game in which we will use different kinds of frowns. Remember the different kinds of frowns we talked about. When I say "Frown," make any kind of frown you please, and hold it until

I say "Straight." This means that you should quickly change from the frown to a straight face.

**Evaluation:**

Was your face stiff when you frowned?
Did your face feel loose when you changed from a frown to a straight face?
What do you think happened?

**Activity:**

THE HARD WHISTLE. The movement in this activity is with the lips, as in whistling, but it is done by tensing the lips vigorously.

**Introduction:**

The discussion can begin by asking how many can whistle. This can be followed by a consideration of what causes the whistling sound.

**Responses:**

The responses can be noisy because those children who can do so are likely to begin immediately to whistle.

**Leader:**

Did you notice the shape of your mouth and lips? They formed a circle. Now, let's try what we will call the hard whistle. What does that suggest to you?

**Responses:**

Children give various comments on the position of the lips in the hard whistle.

**Leader:**

Let's try the hard whistle, when I say "Whistle." When I say "Stop," let your lips go back to the regular position.

**Evaluation:**

What kind of feeling did you have on your mouth and lips when you did the hard whistle?

Did your lips feel tight?
How did they feel when you stopped?

## Muscles of the Upper Extremities

**Activity:**

THE SQUEEZER. This activity involves squeezing an imaginary object. It is simply concerned with making a tightly clenched fist and then releasing to an open hand.

**Introduction:**

The discussion can start with the leader asking what is meant by the word squeeze, how the squeeze is accomplished, and under what conditions it is done.

**Responses:**

Children will give all sorts of responses, some of which include the following:
You squeeze lemons.
You squeeze tight on a bat when hitting a ball.
I like to squeeze a toothpaste tube.
I once squeezed a cherry and the seed popped out.

**Leader:**

There are certainly many things to squeeze and ways to squeeze them. The kind of squeeze I am thinking about is one in which you would use your whole hand to squeeze something, let's say like a small rubber ball. Let's try it. When I say "Squeeze," everyone pretend to squeeze something in your hand. You can use both hands to pretend you have something in each hand. Then I will say "Open," and you can stop squeezing and let your hand come open.

**Evaluation:**

Did your hands get tired when you squeezed hard? How did it feel when I said "Open?"

**Activity:**

**THE RUBBER BAND.** One way to be like a rubber band is to clasp the hands tightly in front of the chest with the elbows pointing out to the sides. The idea of the rubber band is shown when the performer tries as hard as possible to pull the hands apart.

**Introduction:**

A discussion can focus on rubber bands and their uses. Different sized rubber bands can be presented and stretched to various lengths. (This is exciting for the children because they wonder if the rubber band is going to break.)

**Responses:**

Children will enter eagerly into a discussion about rubber bands because practically all of them will have had some sort of experience with them.

**Leader:**

I wonder how it would feel to be a rubber band and stretch like one? Let's try some movements that would make us be like a rubber band.

**Responses:**

Children do a large variety of movements, depicting a rubber band.

**Leader:**

I noticed that some of you held your hands together like your arms were a rubber band. (If this does not happen, it could possibly be suggested by the leader.) Let's try to stretch the rubber band until it breaks. When I say "Start," try to stretch very hard like a rubber band. When I say "Snap," pretend that the rubber band breaks.

**Evaluation:**

Did your arms get tired quickly when you were stretching them like a rubber band? Did your hands and arms feel tight? How did it feel when I said "Snap?"

**Activity:**

**THE WEIGHT LIFTER.** This activity is concerned with lifting an imaginary weight, while at the same time straining, as if actually lifting a heavy weight. The kind of lift thought of here is known as the "curl." The lifter stands upright. The weight is on the floor in front. The performer bends at the knees, stoops, and picks up the weight with both hands, "curling" it to the chest.

**Introduction:**

The discussion can be introduced by asking what is meant by the term *weight lifter.*

**Responses:**

Since weight lifting has become a popular event, many children will have seen the activity on television. They are very interested in the strength it takes to lift the heavy weights.

**Leader:**

(The discussion is focused on various ways to lift weights with emphasis on the curl.) What do you think we mean when we say that one way of lifting a weight is the curl?

**Responses:**

Some children will know immediately, and the discussion can be directed to why it is called the curl. (Weight is curled by the arms up to the chest.)

**Leader:**

Let's see if we can be weight lifters and try to curl. When I say "Curl," pretend you are lifting a heavy weight. When I say "Stop," pretend to drop the weight.

**Evaluation:**

Did your arms feel tight when you were lifting the weight? Did your arms get a tired feeling? How did it feel when the weight was dropped?

### Muscles of the Lower Extremities

**Activity:**

**ANKLE SNAP.** In this activity the ankle is flexed (bent) very hard toward the body in order to stretch the muscles at the back of the legs from the knee down. This position is held for a short period, and then the foot is extended outward for a short period. Finally, the position is released, relaxing the muscles. Each ankle can be flexed and extended separately.

**Introduction:**

The discussion can center around the various extremities of the body with reference to how the different kinds of joints can bend (be flexed). The activity can be named, and the leader can ask what they think is meant by it.

**Responses:**

The kind of introduction mentioned above will likely result in many kinds of responses indicating experiences children have had with various body joints.

**Leader:**

(The leader takes into account the different responses and then attempts to direct these to the activity.) You have suggested many things that can be done with the ankles. Could you show us some of these things?

**Responses:**

Children react with different ankle movements. If the leader notices a movement similar to the ankle snap, this is pointed out.

**Leader:**

Let's play the ankle snap game. When I say "Stretch in," try to do this, and when I say "Stretch out," try to do that. When I say "Snap," quickly stop stretching the ankle.

**Evaluation:**

Did you stretch as hard as you could? How did it feel? Did you feel a change when I said "Snap?" How did that feel?

**Activity:**

KICK UP. This activity is best accomplished from a sitting position in a chair or the edge of a desk or table. The sitting position should be such that the edge is under the knee. One leg is extended and held for a short period. The extended leg should be very stiff. After the short period, the leg is allowed to bend back to the original position. Each leg can be extended separately.

**Introduction:**

The discussion can begin by asking about kicking as a movement. Particular reference can be made to its use as a skill in certain kinds of activities.

**Responses:**

Children are likely to mention games in which the skill of kicking is used, such as football, soccer, and the popular game of kickball played in many schools.

**Leader**

(After the discussion about kicking in general, the question is raised about kicking from a sitting position.)

**Responses:**

This will, of course, evoke many different reactions because children will not be likely to think of kicking being used in this manner.

**Leader:**

There is an activity called the kick up. What does this mean to you? Let's try it. When I say "Kick up," will you please do so, and hold it until I say "Down."

**Evaluation:**

How did it feel to kick up? Did your leg feel stiff? Did your leg get tired when you held it up? How did it feel when I said "Down?"

In summary, it should be mentioned that all of the activities presented here have been tested with many children in different kinds of situations. They have met with a great deal of success as a means of relieving tension, and thus, of helping to reduce stress.

The activities for creative relaxation that have been suggested should be considered as representative examples of an almost unlimited number of possibilities. These activities have numerous possible variations that will be immediately noticed by most readers. Therefore, it is recommended that these activities be used as a starting point for the development of other movements for creative relaxation.

# CHAPTER 10

# CONTROLLING STRESS
# THROUGH MEDITATION

The Eastern art of meditation dates back more than 2000 years. Until recently, this ancient art has been encumbered with religious as well as cultural connotations. In the 1960s, counter cultures began using it as a route to a more natural means of living and relaxing. Today, persons from all walks of life can be counted among the untold numbers around the world who practice and realize the positive effects that meditation can have upon the human mind and body. In this final chapter we will take into account various aspects of meditation, including some of the scientific evidence that supports the use of meditation as a stress reduction technique, along with information about a procedure that can be easily learned and practiced for the purpose of controlling stress. Consideration will be given to how adults can practice meditation, and how it can be used effectively to control stress in children.

It has been asserted by Kenneth Pelletier[1] that meditation should be defined as an experimental exercise involving an individual's actual attention, not belief systems or other cognitive processes, and that it should not be confused with prolonged, self-induced lethargy. The nervous system needs intensity and variety of external stimulation to maintain proper functioning.

In the two previous chapters, we were concerned with deep muscle relaxation while the present chapter involves "mind" relaxation. In deep muscle relaxation it is theorized that if the muscles of the body are relaxed, the mind in turn will quiet. The theory involved in meditation is that if the mind is quieted, then

---

[1]Pelletier, Kenneth R., *Mind As Healer Mind As Slayer,* New York, Dell Publishing Co., Inc., 1977, p. 192.

other systems of the body will tend to become stabilized. In this particular regard one authoritative source[2] suggests that at the very least meditation can give the mind a rest—a brief vacation from stress and worry, one that requires neither a travel agent nor days free from the responsibility of work or family. It is almost as though meditation allows us to temporarily shut down those information-processing mechanisms of the brain that are ultimately responsible for producing stress. In addition, this short vacation from stress rests and revitalizes our coping abilities, giving us a more balanced outlook and increased energy for dealing with whatever difficulties face us.

Although there are many meditation techniques, *concentration* is a very essential factor contributing to success. The mind's natural flow from one idea to another is quieted by the individual's concentration. Lowering mental activity may be an easy task, but almost total elimination of scattered thoughts takes a great deal of time and practice on the part of the meditator.

The question sometimes raised is: Are sleep and meditation the same thing? Sleep has been likened to meditation, as both are hypometabolic states; that is, restful states where the body experiences decreased metabolism. But meditation is not a form of sleep. Although some similar psychological changes have been found in sleep and meditation, they are not the same and one is not a substitute for the other. In this regard, it is interesting to note that various studies have shown that meditation may restore more energy than sleep.

There have been countless positive pronouncements about meditation from some of the most notable scientists of modern times who spend a good portion of their time studying about stress. However, it has been in relatively recent years only that the scientific community has uncovered many of the positive effects that the repeated practice of meditation has upon those who are stress ridden. Various scientific studies have shown that meditation can actually decrease the possibilities of an individual contracting stress-related disorders, and that meditators have a much

[2]Woolfolk, Robert L., and Richardson, Frank C., *Stress, Survival & Sanity*, New York, The New American Library, Inc., 1978, p. 141.

faster recovery rate when exposed to a stressful situation than non-meditators. Specifically, from a physiological point of view, Herbert Benson[3] has found that meditation decreases the body's metabolic rate, with the following decreases in bodily function involved: (1) oxygen consumption, (2) breathing rate, (3) heart rate and blood pressure, (4) sympathetic nervous system activity, and (5) blood lactate (a chemical produced in the body during stressful encounters). Also, meditation tends to increase the psychological stability of those who practice it, as well as to reduce anxiety. Research seems to be disclosing that meditation can be a path to better health. (Later in the chapter we will examine some of this scientific inquiry in more detail.)

## TYPES OF MEDITATION

Although there are many meditation techniques, one notable stress researcher, Daniel Goleman[4] has stated that research tends to show that one technique is about as good as another for improving the way we handle stress.

Of the various types of meditation, transcendental meditation is by far the best known. It was introduced into the United States several years ago by Mararishi Mahesh Yogi. It is believed that he used the term *transcendental* (a literal meaning of which is "going beyond") to indicate that it projects one beyond the level of a wakeful experience to a state of profound rest along with heightened alertness.[5]

Transcendental meditation involves the repetition of a *mantra* (a word or specific sound) for 15 to 20 minutes daily with the meditator in a relaxed position with closed eyes. Almost without exception those who have practiced transcendental meditation attest to its positive effects. While other forms of meditation may have

---

[3]Benson, Herbert, *The Relaxation Response*, New York, William Morrow and Company, 1975, p. 68.

[4]Goleman, Daniel J., "Meditation Helps Break the Stress Spiral," *Psychology Today*, February 1976.

[5]Bloomfield, Harold H., et al, *TM Discovering Inner Energy and Overcoming Stress*, Boston, G. K. Hall & Co., 1976, p. 7.

specific procedures, it is safe to say that most derive in some way from basic transcendental meditation.

## SCIENTIFIC EVIDENCE SUPPORTING BENEFITS OF MEDITATION FOR ADULTS

The phonomenon of meditation is not an easy one to study objectively. One of the primary reasons for this is that it is extremely difficult to control all the variables inherent in a given situation. For example, the difference in length of meditation sessions as well as the degree of meditating experience of the subjects sometimes militates against obtaining researchable experimental and control groups. These limitations should be kept in mind when reading the following research reports. It should also be remembered that a very large number of studies in this area have been undertaken over the years. Those cited here are merely representative samples of this vast number.

In studying meditation as an intervention in stress reactivity, Daniel Goleman and G. E. Schwartz[6] used skin conductive measures (a process similar to the polygraph—lie detector) to study certain aspects of meditation. There were 60 subjects, 30 of whom had over two years of experience with transcendental meditation. The other 30 were non-meditators. The subjects were randomly selected for participation in one of three conditions: (1) meditation, (2) relaxation with open eyes, and (3) relaxation with closed eyes. In the meditation group both meditators and nonmeditators were assigned. The meditators with experience engaged in transcendental meditation and those without experience (controls) were instructed in a simple version of transcendental meditation. After practicing this for a period of 20 minutes, subjects were instructed to open their eyes and view a five-minute film designed to be used as a stressor. During meditation and while viewing the film, the subjects were measured for skin conductance and pulse rate. These measurements were recorded twice each minute. Experienced meditators showed more increase in skin conductance during the time

---

[6]Goleman Daniel J., and Schwartz, G. E., "Meditation as Intervention is Stress Reactivity," *Journal of Consulting and Clinical Psychology,* 44, 1976.

immediately before the highly emotionally-charged part of the film. However, there was a decrease in this measurement after the film was viewed. These results could be interpreted to mean generally that those experienced in the practice of meditation can relieve stress by using this particular medium.

To study the physiological effects of meditation, R. K. Wallace[7] used as subjects 15 college students who had practiced meditation for a period of from six months to three years. The subjects sat with open eyes for five minutes. This was followed by 15 minutes with closed eyes, and then for a one-half hour period they used transcendental meditation. At the end of this time, they sat with closed eyes for ten minutes followed by open eyes for five minutes.

Several physiological measurements were recorded during transcendental meditation and the control periods. For the experimental period (TM), there was reduction in oxygen consumption by 16 percent. In addition, there was a 14 percent reduction in carbondioxide elimination. These results were interpreted to mean that there was slowed metabolic rate and a state of deep rest. The research also made a comparison of the oxygen consumption reduction during meditation with a night's sleep, and this amounted to a difference of about nine percent. This seemed to justify a generalization that 20 minutes of meditation produced nearly two times the metabolic decrease during sleep. This could also be interpreted to mean that a deep state of relaxation could be obtained in a relatively short period of time by use of meditation.

Since much credence has been placed on stress reduction in the control and resistance to disease, it seems appropriate to look at the specific technique of meditation in this regard. In consideration of the fact that the health of one's gums is assumed to be an acceptable criterion for overall health, and further, that gum inflammation seems related to stress levels, this condition appears to be a satisfactory medium for studying the general area of disease

---

[7]Wallace, R. K., "Physiological Effects of Transcendental Meditation, *Science*, 167, 1970.

resistance. Ira Klemons[8] undertook a study of this nature by examining 46 practicing meditators for common inflammation of the gums before and after a special course involving extended meditation. Significant improvement was reported for meditators when compared to a control group of non-meditators. A conclusion that could be drawn is that a meditation program increases resistance to disease if, as mentioned previously, gum inflammation can be accepted as a valid criterion.

## A PROCEDURE FOR MEDITATING FOR ADULTS

We are presenting here a description of a procedure for meditating that we have found has met with personal success. In addition, many of our students have reported success with its use. However, it should be mentioned that is is pretty much an individual matter, and what may be successful for one person may not necessarily be successful for another.

To begin with, there are certain basic considerations that should be taken into account. The following descriptive list of these considerations is general in nature, and the reader can make his or her own specific application as best fits individual needs and interests.

**Locate a quiet place and assume a comfortable position.** The importance of a quiet environment should be obvious since concentration is facilitated in a tranquil surrounding. The question of the position one may assume for meditation is an individual matter. However, when it is suggested that one assume a comfortable position, this might be amended by "but not too comfortable." The reason for this is that if one is too comfortable there is the possibility of falling asleep, and this of course would defeat the purpose of meditation. This is a reason why one should consider not taking a lying position while meditating.

A position might be taken where there is some latitude for "swaying." This can provide for a comfortable posture and, at the same time, guard against the individual's "falling into dreamland."

---

[8]Klemons, Ira M., Change in Inflammation in Persons Practicing Trancendental Meditation Technique (Pennsylvania State University, University Park, Pennsylvania) *Scientific Research on the Transcendental Meditation Program: Collected Papers*, Vol. 1, ed. David W. Orme-Johnson and John T. Farrow, New York: MIU Press, 1975.

The main consideration is that the person be in a comfortable enough position to remain this way for a period of at least 15 minutes or so. One such position would be where you sit on the floor with legs crossed and back straight and resting on the legs and buttocks. The head should be erect and the hands resting in the lap. If you prefer to sit in a chair rather than on the floor, select a chair with a straight back. You need to be the judge of comfort, and, thus, you select a position where you feel you are able to concentrate and remain in this position for a period of time.

**Focus your concentration.** As mentioned before, concentration is the essential key to successful meditation. If you focus on one specific thing, such as an object or sound or a personal feeling, it is less likely that your thoughts will be distracted. You might want to consider focusing on such things as a fantasy trip, re-experiencing a trip already taken, a place that has not been visited, or a certain sound or chant.

**Use of a nonsense word or phrase.** Some techniques of meditation such as the popular transcendental meditation, involve the chanting of a particular word (mantra) as one meditates. While the mantra has important meaning for the meditator, we refer to it as a nonsense word because it should be devoid of any connotation that would send one thinking in many directions. This, of course, would hinder concentration, so a nonsense word would perhaps be most effective. Incidentally, we have found that in our own personal experience with meditation, the practice of chanting such a word is very effective.

**Be aware of natural breathing rhythm.** The importance of natural breathing rhythm should not be underestimated. In fact, some clinical psychologists recommend this as a means of concentrating. That is, one can count the number of times he or she inhales and exhales, and this in itself is a relaxing mental activity.

**The time for meditation.** Since meditation is an activity to quiet the mind we strongly recommend that the practice not be undertaken immediately upon arrival home from work. At this time, the mind may be in a very active state of reviewing the day's activities. Our own personal experience suggests a 15 to 20 minute period in the morning before work, and another such period in the evening preferably before dinner, or possibly two hours after dinner.

With the above basic considerations in mind, you should be ready to experiment. To begin with, assume a comfortable position in a quiet place with as passive an attitude as possible. Try to dismiss all wandering thoughts from your mind and concentrate on a relaxed body while keeping the eyes closed. When feeling fairly relaxed, the repetition of the nonsense word or phrase can begin. This can be repeated orally or silently; that is, through the mind. Repeat your chosen word or phrase in this manner over and over, keeping the mind clear of any passing thoughts. At first, this may be difficult, but with practice, it becomes easier.

After a period of about 15 to 20 minutes have passed, discontinue repetition of the word or phrase. Become aware of your relaxed body once again. Give yourself a few moments before moving as your body will need to readjust. For successful prolonged results one might consider continuing the practice two times daily for 15 to 20 minute sessions.

If you have difficulty trying to meditate on your own, it is possible to seek the services of an experienced meditator for assistance and supervision. The recent widespread popularity of meditation has been accompanied by the establishment of meditation centers for instruction in some communities.

## MEDITATION FOR CHILDREN

There is a great deal of available evidence to support the idea that the practice of meditation is very beneficial for children. All family members can learn meditation techniques, and children as young as ten years of age can learn, though they meditate for less than 15 minutes. Often, younger children become interested in learning to meditate after others in the family have begun practicing the technique.

In Hartford, Connecticut, courses in the technique of transcendental meditation have been prepared for primary level children and implemented by some teachers. Among other things, it is reported that this program improves creativity, and that perhaps child psychologists should investigate the effect of the children's technique of transcendental meditation on early development and creativity. With regard to the latter John Gowan[9] studied the facilitation of creativity through meditation. He reviewed the emerging concepts of creativity along with therapeutic procedures designed to relieve the mental blocks caused by anxiety and stress. Various research studies on the use of transcendental meditation to increase creativity, decrease anxiety and control stress suggested that children could be helped to obtain greater creativity through knowledge of one or more meditation techniques.

Work by Deborah Rozman[10] based on actual experiences in teaching the science of meditation to children ages 3–13 has been shown to help make group work with children peaceful, integrated and meaningful. In addition, children are assisted to resolve personal problems and stresses. Moreover, meditation can be used successfully with gifted, retarded, average or hyperactive children.

### Meditation and Attention of Children

Some very interesting research has been done with regard to attentiveness of children. Maureen Murdock[11] describes an approach used by an elementary school teacher to teach meditation exercises to a class of 25 normal and highly gifted kindergarten children. Breathing exercises and the tensing and loosening of muscles were used before going into the process of meditation. Feedback from children themselves seemed to suggest increased levels of attention span.

In another study involving attention, David Redfering[12] had 18 children 8–11 years olds participate in either the treatment group and practice Herbert Benson's meditative-relaxation tech-

[9]Gowan, John Curtis, "The Facilitation of Creativity Through Meditation Procedures," *Journal of Creative Behavior,* 12(3), 1978, p. 156–160.

[10]Rozman, Deborah, *Meditating with Children: A Workbook on New Age Educational Methods Using Meditation,* Boulder Creek, California, University of the Trees Press, 1976.

[11]Murdock, Maureen H., "Meditation with Young Children," *Journal of Transpersonal Psychology,* Vol. 10(1), 1978, p. 29–44.

[12]Redfering, David L., "Effects of Meditative-Relaxation Exercise on Non-Attending Behaviors of Behaviorally Disturbed Children," *Journal of Clinical Psychology,* 1981 Summer Vol. 10(2), p. 126–127.

nique or in the non-treatment group, relaxing for the same 20-minute sessions over a five-day period. Non-attending behavioral levels were recorded during the treatment period. Mean change differences of non-attending behaviors for the two groups reflected a significant reduction in the number of non-attending behaviors for the treatment group.

A study concerned with attention deficit disorder with hyperactivity was conducted by Jonathan Kratter and John Hogan.[13] A total of 24 children, meeting several criteria for being diagnosed as having an attention deficit disorder with hyperactivity, were selected for the study. Children were assigned to one of three conditions: a meditation-training group, a progressive-muscle-relaxation group, or a waiting list control group. Subjects in the training groups were seen on an individual basis for 20 minutes twice weekly for a period of four weeks. Meditating subjects sat with eyes closed, breathed slowly, and deeply, and repeated the Sanskrit word "ahnam" ("nameless") first aloud and then silently for periods gradually increasing in duration from two to eight minutes. Relaxing subjects tensed and relaxed hands, forearms, biceps, triceps, shoulders, stomach, thighs, and calves in periods increasing from two to eight minutes. Results indicated that both the meditation-training and relaxation-training groups showed significant decreases in levels of impulsivity. No change in impulsivity was found in the control group. In the measures of selective deployment of attention and freedom from distractibility, only meditation training resulted in a significant improvement in the behavior of children in both the meditation-training and relaxation-training groups. Parent rating scales reflected a significant improvement in the behavior of children in both the meditation-training and relaxation-training groups.

---

[13]Kratter. Jonathan and Hogan, John D., "The Use of Meditation in the Treatment of Attention Deficit Disorder with Hyperactivity," *RIE*. December 1983.

## Meditation and Child Learning

Over a period of several years, the present authors have been involved in extensive research in the general area of child learning and development. Consequently, an appreciable amount of time has been spent in sorting out some of the research concerned with the effectiveness of meditation upon these areas. The first study of this general nature reported here involves reaction time and meditation and was conducted by Robert Shaw and David Kolb.[14]

Reaction time is the amount of time it takes from the time a signal is given until the initial movement (stimulus-response). This should not be confused with speed of movement, which is concerned with how fast the initial movement is completed.

In this study the subjects were nine meditators with a like number of non-meditators as controls. All subjects reacted to a signal that was a flash of light. At this stimulus the subjects responded by pressing a button. The results showed that meditators tended to react faster than non-meditators by almost a 30 percent difference. Following such stimulus-response trials, all subjects took a 15 minute break period. During this time the meditators practiced transcendental meditation and the non-meditators sat with eyes closed. On a retest of both groups, the meditators' reaction time increased by about ten percent.

Various generalizations could be drawn from this study. For example, one could be tempted to conclude that practicing meditation could improve coordination of mind and body.

The extent to which reaction time can be considered to be associated with learning is not entirely clear. However, it is interesting to note that some Russian investigators have speculated that if children practice activities that involve the use of reaction time, their reading ability will improve. If this is the case, and if meditation increases reaction time, then the question might be raised

---

[14]Shaw, Robert and Kolb, David, "One Point Reaction Time Involving Meditators and Non-Meditators," (University of Texas, Austin) *Scientific Research on the Transcendental Meditation Program: Collected Papers*, Vol. 1, ed. David A. Orme-Johnson and John T. Farrow, New York, MIU Press, 1975.

with regard to the use of meditation with children as a means of helping them improve in reading.

The next study, conducted by Karen Blasdell[15] involved the use of meditation and perceptual-motor performance. Before commenting on the results of this research, it seems appropriate to discuss some general aspects of perceptual-motor development. *Perception* is concerned with how we obtain information from the environment through the various sensory modalities and what we make of it. The term *motor* is concerned with the impulse for motion resulting in a change in position through the various forms of body movement. When the two terms are put together (perceptual-motor) the implication is an organization of interpretation of sensory data, with related voluntary motor responses.

Perceptual-motor training attempts to correct various types of child learning disabilities that may stem from an impairment of the central nervous system and/or have their roots in certain social or emotional problems of children. Through the medium of perceptual-motor development there is said to be correction, or at least some degree of improvement, of certain motor deficiencies, especially those associated with fine motor coordination. What some specialists have identified as a "perceptual-motor deficit" syndrome is said to exist with certain neurologically handicapped children. An attempt may be made to correct or improve fine motor control problems through a carefully developed sequence of motor competencies, which follow a definite hierarchy of development.

What then are the perceptual-motor skills? Generally, the kind of skills that fit into a combination of manual coordination and eye-hand skills may be considered a valid classification. Theoretically, improvement in such skills will be accompanied by an increase in academic achievement.

Now, back to the work of Blasdell, who investigated the influence of meditation on perceptual-motor coordination. She had a group of 15 meditators and a control group of non-meditators

[15]Blasdell, Karen S., "The Effects of the Transcendental Meditation Technique Upon a Complex Perceptual-Motor Task," (University of California, Los Angeles) *Scientific Research on the Transcendental Meditation Program; Collected Papers,* Vol. 1, ed., David W. Orme-Johnson and John T. Farrow, New York, MIU Press, 1975.

participate in a complex perceptual-motor task using the Mirror-Star Tracing Test. This test measures the ability to trace a pattern while looking at its reflection in a mirror without being disoriented. Her results indicated that the meditators demonstrated much greater eye-hand coordination in ability to handle the task faster and more accurately than the non-meditators.

From this study, one could draw the conclusion that meditating could have a profound influence on perceptual-motor performance. If there is any credence to the notion that improved perceptual-motor performance results in improved academic achievement, then the value of meditation in this connection is readily discerned. However, it should be mentioned that research is not conclusively supportive of the idea that improved perceptual-motor performance will always result in better academic achievement. This is to say that some studies are supportive of the theory while others are not. Nevertheless, the use of meditation in this area should continue to be explored.

In a study concerned with learning disabilities, Yvonne Jackson[16] hypothesized that transcendental meditation can be effective in alleviating learning disorders and enhancing the learning process. Sixteen Black low-income adolescents in an urban school system were tested. Instruments included the Personal Orientation Inventory, Gray Oral Reading Tests, and the Wide Range Achievement Test. Results indicated that meditation increased the three personality measures of other/inner-directed, self-regard, and acceptance of aggression. Trends toward improvement in reading and arithmetic achievement were also evident.

In the field of special education, Phillip Ferguson[17] reviewed research on the physiological, perceptual and psychological benefits of the practice of transcendental meditation for potential applicability to exceptional children. Meditation was seen to be of importance to education in that it is reported to improve learning,

---

[16]Jackson, Yvonne, Learning Disorders and the Transcendental Meditation Program: Retrospects and Prospects, a Preliminary Study with Economically Deprived Adolescents, Doctoral Dissertation, University of Massachusetts, *Dissertation Abstracts International*, Ann Arbor, Michigan, Univ. M-films, No. 77-26425.

[17]Ferguson, Phillip C., "Transcendental Meditation and Its Potential Application in the Field of Special Education," *Journal of Special Education*, Vol. 10, No. 2, Summer, 1976.

memory, grades, interpersonal relationships and cognitive perceptual functioning. It is suggested that meditation would be applicable to exceptional or developmentally disabled children.

In an extensive study of mentally retarded Korean children, Dong-Keuk Kim[18] used Yoga exercises and dieting over a five-year period with 240 children with mental defects. The regimen also included *meditation,* physical training and breathing exercises. The program helped to restore emotional stability and control behavior in addition to enhancing physical posture. The number of problems decreased by about 60 percent. A general increase in scholastic performance was noticed. Participating teachers and parents also profited from Yoga exercise and dieting.

We mention this study because meditation has long been an important concomitant ally with Yoga exercises. Rachel Carr,[19] one of the foremost authorities on·Yoga exercises for children, considers meditation a very important "mental exercise" and feels that it can make a child a more understanding and considerate person. She suggests that a child sit in a quiet place where he or she will not be disturbed and begin to relax the mind by breathing quietly with eyes closed. She asks children to concentrate on the rhythm of breathing so as to feel the breath rise and fall while inhaling and exhaling through the nostrils. While listening to the breath, the mind is turned inward and children are asked to meditate on the following five principles:

1. Silence: When you are silent, you will still your mind.
2. Listening: When you listen, you learn.
3. Remembering: When you remember, you become more considerate of others.
4. Understanding: When you understand, your actions will have more meaning.
5. Acting: Finally, when you act, it should be with a gentle heart and an understanding mind. Only then can you truly say that you are able to forgive those who have harmed you, and that you are a better person for it.

---

[18]Kim, Dong-Keuk, *The Mentally Retarded and Yoga,* Report of the Second Asian Conference on Mental Retardation, Tokyo, Japan League for the Mentally Retarded, 1975.

[19]Carr, Rachel, *Wheel, Camel, Fish, and Plow Yoga for You,* Englewood Cliffs, New Jersey, Prentice-Hall, Inc., 1981, p. 29–30.

The studies reported here comprise but a few of the large number that have been undertaken in the area of effectiveness of meditation for children. In all cases, these examples have shown a very positive effect of meditation. However, we repeat that certain precautions need to be taken into account in interpreting the results, and we remind the reader again of the limitations that were mentioned at the outset of this discussion.

In closing this chapter, we would like to mention a television program that we observed recently. The program was called: "Special Treat: Feel Like Dancin'?" At the end of the program some of the children were asked to give their reaction to it. One boy, perhaps nine or ten years of age, said, "It's a bit like meditation; you let your spirit fun free."

All of the recommendations made throughout the book have met with varying degrees of success with adults and children who have practiced them. Individual differences indicate that one person may find more success than another with a given procedure. One of the most important factors to take into account is that controlling stress in children as well as adults is an individual matter. With practice, most adults will have some degree of success in their attempts to control their own stressful conditions as well as those of children with whom they are associated. Above all, a positive attitude toward life in general is an essential prerequisite for controlling stress and this should be instilled in children early in their lives.

# INDEX